W. Maxwell
90s-h
G-15

GREAT
IS THE LORD

GREAT
IS THE LORD

by

Robert G. Lee

FLEMING H. REVELL COMPANY

Printed in the United States of America

LIBRARY OF CONGRESS CATALOG CARD NUMBER: 55-5393

Westwood, N.J.—316 Third Avenue
Los Angeles 41—2173 Colorado Boulevard
London E.C. 4—29 Ludgate Hill
Glasgow C. 2—229 Bothwell Street

CONTENTS

I   Christ or Condemnation   9

II   Consequences of Man's Alliance with Satan .   .   33

III   Justification   58

IV   Forgetting Things Behind   76

V   Declared Directions   93

VI   Great Is the Lord   109

VII   Jesus Coming to Earth Again   132

GREAT
IS THE LORD

I

CHRIST OR CONDEMNATION

He that believeth on him is not condemned: but he that believeth not is condemned already, because he hath not believed in the name of the only begotten Son of God
(John 3:18).
He that believeth on the Son hath everlasting life: and he that believeth not the Son shall not see life; but the wrath of God abideth on him (John 3:36).

As to where these words are found, consider:

1. The Place: These words hold the friendship of heaven and the hostilities of hell, the splendors of a glorified noon and the terrors of a black midnight of shuddering earthquake and destructive tornado. They give forth the assembled fragrance of flower gardens of love and the sulphur fumes of the pits of perdition. These words—continents of truth compressed into a corner of language—are summer's cooling breezes and thunder cloud's wrath in one voice. These words, God's Gospel organs in one diapason, comprehend in themselves the salvation of all who believe on the Lord Jesus Christ and assert the damnation of all who refuse to believe on Christ "Who gave himself for us that he might redeem us from all iniquity, . . ." (Titus 2:14). These words—sweet as a mother's lullaby to a fretful child, solemn as the jury's findings of guilt without recommendation to mercy—set forth the issues of life and death.

These words—like the voice of the morning stars when they sang together and like the voice of a cataract of illimitable rage, full of love as when a maiden whispers her vows of fidelity and like the voice of

9

anguish of a woman in travail—are like joy-bells crossed with death-bells in our ears. These weighty words—like clouds that drench drouth-plagued fields with refreshing rains and like clouds that bruise and blast with heavy hailstones—breathe the language of eternity. These words—soothing the believing heart as the echo of distant music soothes the ear, and disturbing the unbelieving heart, as the wail of despair from some leper in his lair disturbs the sleeper's rest at night—set forth eternal life and the doom and gloom of eternal death.

And we should listen to these words of promise and warning as slaves listen to an emancipation proclamation or as children frightened at the roar of a storm—because these solemn words, pointing to heaven and to hell, are forever fixed in the Word of God. These words are not the ponderings of philosophers or the mere memoirs of men. Therefore, they are certain—certain as that light and heat come and go with the sun. No "probably" or "perhaps" or "maybe" has kinship with them. These words are true—not false like malice in the mouth of envy, like the adulterate promises of a demagogue, like the fowler's artful snare. These words are not phantasmagoric—like a mirage beyond the horizon. These words, pointing out the way to life and giving warning against the way of death, are not imaginative—like the fictions of novelists. These words are not the immature conclusions and shallow judgments of pseudo-psychologists and myth writers. No. They hold wisdom which "excelleth folly as far as light excelleth darkness." They are the Word of God—with credentials clear—marked with the seal of high divinity. On them the signature of God is indelibly stamped.

The place in which these words are found is the Bible—the one Book inspired in totality by the Holy Spirit, regenerative in power, infallible in authority, harmonious in infinite complexity, inexhaustive in adequacy, miraculous as to diversity in unity.

In the matter of the most tremendous issue of any life—the salvation of man's soul—a most appalling contrast do these words set forth. "For God sent not his Son into the world to condemn the world; but that the world through him might be saved" (John 3:17).

"He that believeth on him is not condemned" (John 3:18). "He that believeth on the Son hath everlasting life" (John 3:36). Glory in these words—the attainment of the soul's greatest need, salvation from sin and its consequences. ". . . but he that believeth not is condemned already, because he hath not believed in the name of the only begotten Son of God" (John 3:18). "He that believeth not the Son shall not see life, but the wrath of God abideth on him" (John 3:36). Hopeless despair and damnation these words set forth. They declare a destiny as different as an equinoctial is from an evangel, as different as a crystal sea from a mud puddle, as different as a sonata of Beethoven on a piano is different from the mournful and raucous monotony of a wheezy saxophone in an idiot's hands, as different as orchid's breath from grocery garlic, as different as a garden's fragrant delight to eyes and nostrils from a dungeon's dark and foulsome depths, as different as harmonious voices of holy mirth to human ears from the hideous voices of maniacal madness and shriek.

"Not condemned." "Everlasting life." Glories beyond words to portray. "Condemned already." "The wrath of God." Horrors eternal, shames endless, woes more dreadful and odious because seen in the light of redemptive love.

The truths of the contrast set forth in these words show the choice man must make—the choosing open to all. Eternal life or the wrath of God confronts all. All men and women *can* choose life or death, heaven or hell—not both. All men and women *do* choose life or death, and heaven or hell—not both. Surely any man who has heard just once that the death of Jesus Christ is the most tremendous evidence of man's sinful condition—any man who despises not the love of God—any man who is not a hopeless fool or utter maniac—will choose eternal life and will through trust in Christ get out from under the wrath of God. Yet many—as those who prefer the world's dunce cap to God's crown of wisdom, as those who throw away diamonds and lay up tinsel as treasure, as those who drink not God's nectar but drain Satan's poison cup, as slaves who refuse eternal life and deliriously choose the wrath of God—many refuse coronation and enthronement and choose the coffin and entombment. Many—

blind as hooded falcons, blinking at God's guiding lights and warning lights like disreputable and drunken owls at the noonday sun—refuse heaven and choose hell. Thus do they prove how foolish men can be in what they refuse and in what they choose—how what they incubate as gold hatched the eggs of the cockatrice.

These words reveal:

2. THE PERPETRATOR—"He that": "He"—the sinner. God, calling a convention of deity, said: "Let us make man in our image, after our likeness: . . ." (Genesis 1:26). Thus man—made a compound of the material universe and the spiritual universe, the dust of the ground and the breath of God—was God's image, created in the righteousness and holiness of truth. Adam was capable of making the deepest and brightest manifestation of God to the whole universe. "God made man upright"—without a defect as a rational and responsible subject of law. But Adam sinned and became the transgressor, setting his will against the will of God.

Thus, in the Edenic paradise where God invited heaven and earth, sin, black as night, entered and drove out the morning splendor —causing the earth henceforth to stand under the shadow of death. In disobedience to God man denied the sovereignty of God and pushed God from the throne of his heart—giving evidence of the rebellion of the individual will of the creature against the Creator's universal order. Adam, federal head of the race, let Satan subvert the constitutional order of his nature, dismantle him of his nobility and bring him into surrender to diabolical power—thus causing him treacherously to yield up the keys of his soul's citadel placed in his keeping.

Thus, because Adam brought death upon himself and all his posterity by an act of rebellion that introduced the leaven of moral disintegration into the harmonious family of worlds and involving countless hosts of unborn creatures in unmeasured misery, transmitting his perpetration of evil to all generations—we read these awful words of truth which show that guilt and punishment by God himself are joined: "Wherefore, as by one man sin entered into the world, and death by sin; and so death passed upon all men, for that all have sinned" (Romans 5:12). Those who dwell on the goodness of God to the disparagement of his justice, build a deity of their own liking which God does not recognize. God says that both Jews and Gentiles—all peoples of all nations of earth—are under sin, that none are righteous, that none understand, that none seek after God, that all have gone out of the way, that all are unprofitable to God, that all are guilty before God of doing not good (Romans 3:9-12).

The universal testimony of the Scriptures is that man by nature, by deed, by thought, by word, is the perpetrator of evil. All men have turned to their own ways. All are unclean—by nature corrupt. Isaiah, the prophet in whose preaching are the thunders and lightnings of Sinai and the foregleams of Calvary, said:

> But we are all as an unclean thing, and all our righteousnesses are as filthy rags; and we all do fade as a leaf; and our iniquities, like the wind, have taken us away. And there is none that calleth upon thy name, that stirreth up himself to take hold of thee: . . . (Isaiah 64: 6-7).

Solomon's words describe the sinful nature of man until this day: "For there is not a just man upon earth, that . . . sinneth not" (Ecclesiastes 7:20). And John by the Holy Spirit wrote: "All unrighteousness is sin . . ." and ". . . we know . . . the whole world lieth in wickedness" (I John 5:17, 19). The indictment from God, the same today as of old, is thus expressed:

> Being filled with all unrighteousness, fornication, wickedness, covetousness, maliciousness; full of envy, murder, debate, deceit, malignity; whisperers, Backbiters, haters of God, despiteful, proud, boasters, inventors of evil things, disobedient to parents, without understanding, covenant breakers, without natural affection, implacable, unmerciful: Who knowing the judgment of God, that they which commit such things are worthy of death, not only do the same, but have pleasure in them that do them (Romans 1:29-32).

Moreover, history and human experience reveal the formidable nature of our common depravity. Frankly we confess the presence and power of the malign force which works to man's undoing. The working of fiercest passions is implicit in all men. A dark dynamic factor disturbs the harmony of the universe, filling it with travail and pain. The story of the hatred, injustice, cruelty, and crimes of the race since Adam plunged into sin is written large in the scarlet pages of the historian. And all the while, the moralist concludes the long chapter of our vices by bitter criticisms of our virtues as so many vices in disguise. History shows how often man has set up his own gods, has bowed down to them, has burned incense to them—forgetting God.

God's head-to-foot, life-size photograph of man portrays man as perpetrator, as sinner—shows how sin has taken possession of different parts of his being—shows how desperately he needs to be made a new creation by the new birth. Examine this photograph carefully, and ask questions about it. What about the head? "The whole head is sick . . ." (Isaiah 1:5). What about the eyes? "Having eyes full of adultery, and that can not cease from sin; . . ." (II Peter 2:14). "There is no fear of God before their eyes" (Romans 3:18). Covetous eyes (Jeremiah 22:17). Idolatrous and evil eyes (Ezekiel 20:24 and Mark 7:22). What about the ears? They are dull of hearing as to spiritual things and disobedient (Matthew 13:15 and Jeremiah 11:18). What about the mouth? It is full of cursing, bitterness, deceit, frauds, vanity (Romans 3:14, Psalms 10:7, 36:3). What about the lips? Poison of asps is under them (Romans 3:13). The lips are lying and contentious, as many Scriptural words state. What about the tongue? It is a fire, a world of iniquity, full of deadly poison (James 3), a scourge (Job 5:21) a sharp sword (Psalms 57:4), and guilty of many evils, as many other Bible words show. What about the throat? It is an open sepulchre (Romans 3:13). What about the neck? It is stiff, rebellious, disobedient, haughty, hardened (Deuteronomy 31:27, Jeremiah 17: 23, Isaiah 3:16). What about the hands? They are full of mischief and bribes and acts of violence, wicked, defiled with blood (Psalms 26:10, Isaiah 1:15). What about the feet? They are the feet of pride (Psalms 36:11). They are feet that are swift in running to mischief (Proverbs 6:18). They are feet that run to evil and hasten to shed blood (Proverbs 1:16 and Romans 3:15). They are feet that go down to death (Proverbs 3:5). What about the bones? They are full of the

sins of youth (Job 20:11). What about the heart? As the seat of the
affections, passions, will, moral character, and spiritual life, it is de-
ceitful above all things and desperately wicked (Jeremiah 17:9).

What about the mind of the sinner? It is reprobate (Romans 1:
8), corrupt (I Timothy 6:5), defiled (Titus 1:15), fleshly (Romans
8:7), blinded (II Corinthians 3:14), hardened in pride (Daniel 5:20).

What about the sinner's thoughts? They are only evil continually
(Genesis 6:5), foolishness (Proverbs 24:9), God not in them (Psalms
10:4).

What about the understanding? It is darkened (Ephesians 4:
18). What about the conscience? It is seared (I Timothy 4:2), defiled
(Titus 1:15), evil (Hebrews 10:22).

Isaiah sums it up: "From the sole of the foot even unto the head
there is no soundness in it; but wounds, and bruises, and putrifying
sores: they have not been closed, neither bound up, neither mollified
with ointment" (Isaiah 1:6).

What a perpetrator man has been since sin threw him, woefully
deranged, miserable, erratic, lost, into interminable leagues of night.
Man's wickedness, since Adam plunged into sin and carried the
whole race with him, has authenticated Bible truth:

> Behold, I was shapen in iniquity; and in sin did my mother conceive
> me (Psalms 51:5).

> The wicked are estranged from the womb: they go astray as soon
> as they be born, speaking lies (Psalms 58:3).

Every person was born with a sinful nature—and you must take it
out or every person born will live in hell. ". . . and were by nature the
children of wrath" (Ephesians 2:3), ". . . without Christ . . . having
no hope, and without God in the world" (Ephesians 2:12). Sin ex-
tends to each member of the human family, singling out each mortal
as its chief protagonist. No member of the race has escaped sin's corruption—or is immune to it. And Jesus, in whom are all the treasures
of divine wisdom, was not guilty of the unparalleled folly of coming
from heaven to the cross to atone for innocent creatures, to reprieve
persons uncondemned, to redeem a race of free men, to revoke the

death sentence where death was not, to expire under the sense of the wrath of God that he might save from hell people in no danger of going to hell. "He that believeth on the Son hath everlasting life: and he that believeth not the Son shall not see life: but the wrath of God abideth on him" (John 3:36). "He that believeth on him is not condemned: but he that believeth not is condemned already, because he hath not believed in the name of the only begotten Son of God" (John 3:18).

Let us consider now:

3. THE PERSON. "The Son." "He that believeth on the Son." "He that believeth not the Son."

Orators use words that are like flights of golden arrows. Poets make archangelic flight through realms of thought. Writers wield pens from whose points truths drop like golden pollen from the stems of shaken lilies. Musicians build rhythmic palaces of melody before the eyes of men's souls.

Philosophers and preachers, with words that glow with truth, like hot coals aflame in darkness, breathe the spiritual across mountains of materialism.

Scientists, with achievements that astound, almost awake in men a primeval faith in magic.

But the best that all these can do when it comes to giving a full portrayal of all that this glorious person, Jesus Christ, is in making a reality God's redemptive purposes and plans, is as man's mean paint on God's fair lily. All their portrayals are as woefully inadequate as the attempt of fumbling fingers to play Beethoven's Ninth Symphony on a cheap tin whistle.

The Son—". . . whom God hath sent, speaketh the words of God . . ." (John 3:34), whom God ". . . hath appointed heir of all things . . ." (Hebrews 1:2)—is He whom "The Father loveth . . . and hath given all things into his hand" (John 3:35). How this brings out the absolute Deity of Jesus Christ! For to none but to One absolutely equal with Himself *could* God give "all things." God is eternal and the Son is co-existent, co-equal, co-eternal, co-essential with God.

Angels are called sons of God; so they are—by creation. Adam was called a son of God; so he was—by creation.

Believers are called sons of God; so they are—by regeneration. But Jesus, the *only* Son of God—the Isaac of his Father—was the Son of eternal generation. Jesus was *the* Son—distinguished from all others. And more easily could I dip up yonder Mississippi with a teaspoon or quickly push yon sun down behind the horizon than could I with words fully portray the Son of God, whom God hath highly exalted and given a name which is above every name, "That at the name of Jesus every knee should bow, of things in heaven, and things in earth, and things under the earth; And that every tongue should confess that Jesus Christ is Lord, to the glory of God the Father" (Philippians 2:10-11).

Jesus, the outstanding miracle of all ages, is the most potent factor in the world's hopes. In Him was no taint of sin, no suspicion of selfishness, no insinuation of an unholy aim. His face was sculptured benevolence. His hand was friendship's symbol. He matched deed with creed, buttressed doctrine with doing, made effective speech with service, blended theory with practice, ever holding up before mankind a representative manhood gloriously conformed to the will of God. He only is our Redeemer. ". . . thou . . . hast redeemed us to God by thy Blood . . ." (Revelations 5:9).

> Neither is there salvation in any other: for there is none other name under heaven given among men, whereby we must be saved (Acts 4:12).

> Christ hath redeemed us from the curse of the law, being made a curse for us: for it is written: Cursed is every one that hangeth on a tree: (Galatians 3:13).

It was necessary that the Redeemer be a God-man. He willingly laid down His life, which He could not have done if He had not been a man. "For such an high priest became us, who is holy harmless, undefiled, separate from sinners, and made higher than the heavens;" (Hebrews 7:26).

He took up His life again, which He could not have done—if He had not been God. The glorious Person of our text is Truth and Life, sinless humanity and holy Deity, so glorious He can not be circumscribed within the poverty of human speech. In the presence of Christ the universal testimony of all saints of all ages has been a confession of humiliation and shame. The word "astronomy" conveys no real picture of the midnight with its oceans of worlds. So all words can not approximate the overpowering grandeur of Christ. Scholars are as bewildered in efforts fully to portray Christ as an owl suddenly flung into a noontide.

But we must give thought to:

4. THE POSSESSION—Everlasting Life: "He that believeth on the Son hath everlasting life . . ." (John 3:36). "He that hath the Son hath life; and he that hath not the Son of God hath not life" (I John 5:12).

The greatest question man has ever asked and has never answered is, "What is Life?" No one can define life. Science has no definition. Laboratories give no answer. Doctors do not know. Graves are silent. Little we know about life. We see life's manifestations—describe some of its effects—but know merely the *fact* of life. Life is in the pulse's beat, the heart's throb, the eye's flash, the thrill of the voice, the smile of lips, the flush of cheeks, the movement of bodies. But, after all, what *is* life?

Everlasting life is not what many call life. Much that people call life is a death's head. A life of worldly gaiety is but death. Paul said "But she that liveth in pleasure is dead while she liveth" (I Timothy 5:6). Everlasting life is not the life of saloonic carousals, of baccarat and billiards, of chasing short-lived butterflies of pleasure, of dancing to the music of self-indulgence, of gambling places with strange fascinations and excitements, of pleasures plentiful as bacteria in bad butter. Not that life is life, but desert breath that drinks up life's dew—as ethereal as the sensuous pallor of waxen candles.

The life mentioned in our text is not the life of fame, the ballroom, the athletic arena, the political battleground, social life with vain display of jewels and fine apparel, the educational realm, military kingdoms, banking worlds. Not that life. But *everlasting* life.

What is eternal life? Can man answer? No. Only God. He answers in His Word:

> And we know that the Son of God is come, and hath given us an understanding, that we may know him that is true, and we are in him that is true, even in his Son Jesus Christ. This is the true God, and eternal life (I John 5:20).

"I am the life," says Jesus—". . . I am the way, the truth, and the life . . ." (John 14:6); ". . . I am . . . the life: he that believeth in me, though he were dead, yet shall he live" (John 11:25). Paul speaks of him as ". . . Christ, who is our life . . ." (Colossians 3:4). Without Christ, you can no more have eternal life than you can have rivers without water or cyclones without wind. "This life is in his Son." Since life is in Christ and we have Christ, then we have what is in Him—*eternal* life. Eternal life is the gift of God. Only God can give such life. Churches, clubs, colleges, culture, education, congresses, can not. Nothing can; nobody can. "For the wages of sin is death; but the gift of God is eternal life through Jesus Christ our Lord" (Romans 6:23). "And walk in love, as Christ also hath loved us, and hath given himself for us an offering and a sacrifice to God for a sweet-smelling savour" (Ephesians 5:2). "And this is the record, that God hath given to us eternal life, and this life is in his Son" (I John 5:11).

Thinking of eternal life, we think of:

5. THE PRICE: "Ye are bought with a price; . . ." (I Corinthians 7:23).

Eternal life is the gift of God, and it cost us nothing. But it cost God much. The price paid was the blood of Christ. ". . . ye were not redeemed with corruptible things, as silver and gold . . . but with the precious blood of Christ . . ." (I Peter 1:18–19). ". . . by his own blood he . . . obtained eternal redemption for us" (Hebrews 9:12). ". . . being now justified by his blood, we shall be saved from wrath through him" (Romans 5:9). To buy us out of the slave markets and bondage of sin Jesus came from the place of worship to the place of wrath—from adoration to agony, from dignity to degradation, from

love to hate, from exaltation to humiliation, from coronation to crucifixion, from heaven's commendation to earth's condemnation, from
the hails of heaven to the nails of the cross, from heaven's throne to
Calvary's tree, from heaven's honors to Golgotha's horrors, from
heaven's glory crown to earth's gory crown, from heaven's glory to
the grave. What a price to pay!

A host of scoffing devils surround His dying bed. The Curse of
the Law is the coverlet over Him. "He was made a curse." The atmosphere He breathes glows with fiery indignation. His last draught,
the distress and agony of a reprobate. The parting hymn sung to Him,
Satanic scoff and scorn, sneer and jeer. His only refuge, His Father's
hidden countenance. "He was made sin." God ordered sin to execu-
tion in the person of His Son. God dealt with Jesus as He must deal
with sin—in severe and unrelenting judgment. That was *the* price!
He the perfectly righteous One, was judged as unrighteous, that we,
the terribly unrighteous ones, might be judged as righteous. "For he
that made him to be sin for us, who knew no sin; that we might be
made the righteousness of God in him" (II Corinthians 5:21).

God came in Christ.

And Christ came in blood.

Choicest mercies came through greatest miseries, pangs, throes
and woes. The wrath of an infinite God beat Him down to the dust.
Not a member or sense of Him but was seat and subject of torment.
He who was the Mercy Seat for the whole world received no mercy
for Himself. He received the wages of sin which He did not earn
that we might receive eternal life which we did not deserve. He was
crushed beneath the weight of the wrath and curse of God. He was
bruised, wounded, numbered with transgressors. He hung where we
ought to have been, and died where we ought to have died. His name
suffered all the vilest indignities, blasphemies and reproaches that
Satan's malignity could utter. Contempt was poured on all His of-
fices, and all for us. That was the price. And now His blood appeases
every storm, heals every wound, blots out every sin, removes every
curse, makes a heavy chain into a gentle yoke.

We are now ready to think of:

6. THE PLIGHT: "Shall not see, shall not have, life."

What a tragic plight! No words can show the horror of such a plight. It means man is *lost*. And *lost* means separation from God, eternal abode in the land of conscious eternal punishment for the impenitent—the opposite of life, love, heaven. It means darkness, not light—bondage, not liberty—ruin, not redemption—damnation, not salvation.

It is the plight of men feeding on devil's corn and choking on the devil's cob, finding out that all Satan's swans are buzzards. It means that sinners choose paper boats for life's voyages.

Oh! Terrible plight of the blind, in a world of light and color! Terrible plight of the deaf, in a world where there are voices and musical instruments. Sad plight of the dumb who would speak— and cannot. Tragic plight of the crippled and maimed who cannot walk. Terrible the plight of lost health, lost honor, lost character. Terrible the plight of those who starve in lands of famine—and of those whose god is their belly in a land of plenty.

Think of the plight of prisoners who, with all the starlit skies and the marvels of the great outdoors, live behind prison bars. Weep over the plight of those who have gone mad.

But no plight of body or mind is as the plight of the sinner, high or low, ignorant or intellectual, who refuses Christ. Any intellectual reason for rejecting HIS life and light ceases to be an excuse; it becomes a crime.

Jesus alone enables us to obtain mercy—and to reach heaven. If He be not gracious to you, vain it is for you to rise early and sit up late to work out your salvation. You gather, and put into a bag with holes—you weave spider's webs which are unfit for clothing—pour into a vessel, the bottom of which is knocked out. But if Jesus is yours, the fruits of peace fall into your lap from the bloody tree you did not plant. You can boast of Christ's righteousness while yet you strive against sin. Your debt in full is paid while you have nothing wherewith to pay—and you can sing:

> My hope is built on nothing less
> Than Jesus' blood and righteousness.

This shows the sinner's helplessness. In its largest sense salvation is the attainment of the soul's greatest need—*God*. A man is lost because through sin he has not holiness—and has, therefore, lost God. That is why God says that the saved man has ". . . escaped the corruption that is in the world through lust" and has become a ". . . partaker of the divine nature . . ." (II Peter 1:4).

Salvation is to be saved from sin and its consequences. Since sin and its consequences consist in a sinful nature and separation from God and liability to penalty, the main elements of salvation are regeneration, pardon, and acceptance with God. And not any of these can the sinner attain for himself. "Not by works of righteousness which we have done, but according to his mercy he saved us, by the washing of regeneration, and renewing of the Holy Ghost" (Titus 3:5). "I, even I, am he that blotteth out thy transgressions for mine own sake, and will not remember thy sins" (Isaiah 43:25). "But when the fullness of the time was come, God sent forth his Son. . . . To redeem them that were under the law, that we might receive the adoption of sons" (Galatians 4:4–5). "For ye are all the children of God by faith in Christ Jesus" (Galatians 3:26). No sinner can pardon himself. God is the offended party—and only God can forget, for all sin and sins are against Him. No sinner can by any means redeem his brother, nor give to God a ransom for Him (Psalms 49:7).

God says: "For as many as are of the works of the law are under the curse: for it is written, Cursed is every one that continueth not in all things which are written in the book of the law to do them" (Galatians 3:10). No sinner can by any acts of his become perfect in the eyes of the law. As every sinner has failed to "continue in all things written in the book of the law to do them," he could not at any time render more than the law demanded—and hence he is doomed to be a moral debtor during all his existence. No sinner can perform a surplusage of obedience to make amends for his derelictions. He can not whittle down the sinfulness of his sin and its penalty—or blow out hell to which sin leads. If the sinner could buy out or resolve out or suffer out the penalty, then "infinite Love has done no marvellous thing in doing what the sinner could and would have done." Christ who is above law, who suffered under law, magnified the law, making the law honorable by obeying its precepts and paying its penalty for men—wrapping up man's destiny with his own—has, for man's salvation, fulfilled the law in its heaviest and most exacting demands against the sinner. "Knowing that a man is not justified by the works of the law, but by the faith of Jesus Christ, even we have believed in Jesus Christ, that we might be justified by the faith of Christ, and not by works of the law: for by the works of the law shall no flesh be justified" (Galatians 2:16). And no sinner can, by any act of his own, regenerate himself. This is a creative act of God's spirit. "Which were born, not of blood, nor of the will of the flesh, nor of the will of man, but of God" (John 1:13). A sinner can as easily fly to the moon on a broomstick as to regenerate himself—because it is a creative act. Man is helpless to save himself by good works.

> For by grace are ye saved through faith; and that not of yourselves: it is the gift of God: (Ephesians 2:8–9).

> Who hath saved us, and called us with an holy calling, not according to our works, but according to his own purpose and grace, which was given us in Christ Jesus before the world began (II Timothy 1:9).

> And if by grace, then is it no more of works: otherwise grace is no more grace. But if it be of works, then is it no more grace: otherwise work is no more work (Romans 11:6).

Man is helpless to save himself by personal and moral righteousness. If we could earn salvation by achieving righteousness, God would owe man salvation as a debt—and it would not be of grace, or unmerited favor.

> For I say unto you, That except your righteousness shall exceed the righteousness of the scribes and Pharisees, ye shall in no case enter into the kingdom of heaven (Matthew 5:20).

> For they being ignorant of God's righteousness, and going about to establish their own righteousness, have not submitted themselves unto the righteousness of God (Romans 10:3).

No man can in himself come up to the standard which God requires
—absolute holiness without which ". . . no man shall see the Lord:"
(Hebrews 12:14). "For whosoever shall keep the whole law, and yet
offend in one point, he is guilty of all" (James 2:10). That means not
only that man is a law breaker and as a law breaker is amenable to
the penalty of the broken law, but that he has sinned against God's
authority which is equal in all law.

But Christ receiveth sinful men, and saves them. "And she shall
bring forth a son, and thou shalt call his name JESUS: for he shall
save his people from their sins" (Matthew 1:21). "For God sent not
his Son into the world to condemn the world; but that the world
through him might be saved" (John 3:17). "But God commendeth
his love toward us, in that, while we were yet sinners, Christ died for
us. Much more then, being now justified by his blood, we shall be
saved from wrath through him" (Romans 5:8-9).

". . . the Lord Jesus Christ our Saviour" (Titus 1:4). "Wherefore
he is able also to save them to the uttermost that come unto God by
him, seeing he ever liveth to make intercession for them" (Hebrews
7:25). "For there is one God, and one mediator between God and
men, the man Christ Jesus; Who gave himself a ransom for all, to be
testified in due time" (I Timothy 2:5-6). "And I give unto them
eternal life; and they shall never perish, neither shall any man pluck
them out of my hand" (John 10:28). Jesus came into the world to
save sinners—not mainly to teach, not chiefly to work miracles, not
primarily to live a beautiful life. These were incidental and collateral
to the one purpose for which He came—to die, "the just for the unjust that He might bring us to God . . ." (I Peter 3:18).

> For the Son of man is come to seek and to save that which was lost
> (Luke 19:10).

> This is a faithful saying, and worthy of all acceptation, that Christ
> Jesus came into the world to save sinners; of whom I am chief (I
> Timothy 1:15).

> And ye know that he was manifested to take away our sins; and in
> him is no sin (I John 3:5).

Herein is love, not that we loved God, but that he loved us, and sent his Son to be the propitiation for our sins (I John 4:10).

There is no other way for the sinner to know and experience redemption rescue except through Jesus who endured the cross and despised the shame, in order that the lawful captive might go free— and the prison doors be opened to those who were bound.

> Could my tears forever flow,
>   Could my zeal no languor know,
>   These for sin could not atone,
>   Thou must save—and Thou alone.
> In my hand no price I bring,
>   Simply to Thy cross I cling.

On the roof of Keble College, Oxford, there is a dragon with its mouth wide open. Standing over the dragon is an angel about to thrust a sword in the shape of a cross down its throat. The thought conveyed to the onlooker's mind is that the cross of our Lord Jesus Christ is the secret of victory over that awful thing, sin, whether considered as a burden pressing heavily upon the conscience, or as a power working within, enslaving. The death of our Lord Jesus Christ, when accepted, delivers from all, the powers of evil within and without. This is absolutely true. To the truth and power of this fact thousands can and do bear glad and joyous testimony.

Now, since we know it was necessary for God to exclude man from His holy presence on account of man's sinful nature, since Christ affirms that man's sinful nature must be regenerated before he can enter into communion with God, and since we know that all human and divine law emphasizes the justice of punishment for transgression, we can now wisely and compassionately give thought to:

7. THE PHRASE—"The wrath of God": This phrase points out horrid and hideous woes. "Wrath of God," for instance. "For the wrath of God is revealed from heaven against all ungodliness and unrighteousness of men, who hold the truth in unrighteousness;" (Romans 1:18). If man had not fallen, such a thing as wrath would not have been revealed. But the self-righteous sinner is treasuring up

wrath for the day of wrath. Since the wrath of God is upon the *contentious* and disobedient (Romans 2:8), since the sinner is by nature a child of wrath (Ephesians 2:3) since the Law of God works wrath (Romans 4:15), since the wrath is to the uttermost (I Thessalonians 2:16), since God warns us to flee from the wrath to come, we rejoice to know that Jesus saves from wrath (Romans 5:9) and delivers from wrath (I Thessalonians 1:10). The whole fight of God from Eden to Calvary was against sin. Man's conduct itself is sufficient to justify the wrath of God against his doings.

The wrath of God! That wrath is the wrath of the Lamb—more terrible than the wrath of the lion. It is the wrath of gentleness against butchery—the wrath of kindness against cruelty, of chastity against unchastity, of truth against falsehood, of light against darkness, of God's righteousness against iniquity, of holiness against sin.

Men have asked: "Can God approve sin—and remit the penalty? Can God ignore sin—and remit the penalty? Can God deny sin—and remit the penalty? Can God admit sin—and yet remit the penalty?" Such is impossible to a righteous God. Calvary is proof of what men would do with God if they could lay hands on Him. Every reader of the Bible knows that it warns men to flee from the wrath to come. Any man who denies the *wrath* of God denies the *Word* of God. Our Lord warned all who reject Him—". . . ye shall die in your sins:" (John 8:24). ". . . Depart from me, ye cursed, into everlasting fire, prepared for the devil and his angels:" (Matthew 25:41). Such words make us tremble. God's wrath is the inevitable reaction of His righteousness and holiness against all sin and guilt—not the reaction of angry, cruel, blood-thirsty passion. God is love and He shows His love—not by taking an unsaved man into heaven but by giving His Son that the sinner might be saved.

In Gethsemane, Christ was in agony from the apprehensions of the wrath of God with which He contested. Ah, what is divine wrath that Christ should faint when the cup came to Him? Could not He bear, and do you think to bear it? Did Christ sweat blood before it, and you think light of it? If it staggered Him, it will confound you. If it made Him groan, it will make you shriek and howl eternally.

See the face of Christ full of purple drops under the sense and appre-
hension of God's wrath. But fools make a mock of sin! (Proverbs
14:9).

Let us now remember that to escape the wrath of God, to come
to the position where our eternal possession will be the virtue and
value of the ransoming work of Christ, give serious thought to:

8. THE PLAN—"Believeth":

"He that *believeth* on the Son hath everlasting life" (John 3:36).
Believeth! To believe Christ is to accept His testimony given in God's
Word as true—to rely upon it under any circumstances whatever—
to be sure that He will do what He has promised, whatever may be
the seeming impossibilities. Saving belief—saving trust, or faith—is
receiving the Lord Jesus Christ into one's own heart as one's own
personal Saviour and Lord and believing that He is there (I John 5:
12). Saving belief is receiving and trusting Him for all that He offers
himself to be—yielding the whole life to His control.

God's plan reveals both the futility and impertinence of our individual and social nostrums that but reveal themselves as tinctures
in the universal poisons. It is most important that we find and be
found of the Christ whose forgivenesses are more than seventy times
seven.

The plan is to *believe* in Christ who was forsaken of God that
He might bring us to God. No man is good enough to be saved—no
man is so bad he can not be saved. No work of righteousness can
merit salvation—if we do not believe. No work of unrighteousness
can forfeit salvation—if we do believe. "For by grace are ye saved
through faith; and that not of yourselves: it is the gift of God:"
(Ephesians 2:8). Salvation is a free gift (Romans 6:23)—one is not
saved *by* works but *for* works. He works *from* the cross not *to* the
cross.

Believe in Christ—and the curse is gone. You are born from
above. You become a child of God and an heir of God. You will receive pardon, be justified in His sight, be counted righteous before
God, be free from condemnation, and have eternal life.

Believe in Him—and the sting of death is extracted.

Believe in Him—and you will have part in the first resurrection.

Believe in Him—and you will have boldness in the day of Judgment.

"Believeth!" That denies salvation by character, refutes salvation by works, contradicts salvation by culture, disproves salvation by feeling and declares salvation by trust.

To reach heaven there is but one place from which to start—Calvary. There is but one way—Christ.

Your wisdom is folly—your virtues, vices—your benevolence, badness—your character, caricature—your religiousness, ruin—your good works, wickedness—your righteousness, iniquity,—if you let them keep you from accepting Christ. Eternal life is through *belief*. How can men and women continue in sin when such infinite happiness and glorious life and glorious heaven is proffered us? Are men's hearts so dead they do not respond to this? It seems so, for some give up Christ for the liquor bottle; some for an atheistic friend; some for an infidelic book; some for a gambler's table; some for an evil woman who hath "cast down many wounded"; some for an ungodly man whose life smells of garbage; some for fame which is like a snowflake on the river—"a moment seen then gone forever"; some for worldly honor; some for political prestige; some for worldly pleasure.

But the questions I have been asking unsaved men through the years are: Did a liquor bottle ever sweat blood in Gethsemane for you? Did a gambler's table offer to reach down and take you out of the horrible pit, and put your feet on a solid rock? Was any atheistic scholar ever crucified for you? Did any infidelic book ever take the scourge for you? Was any ungodly companion—male or female—ever crowned with thorns for you? Did worldly fame or political prestige ever endure shame and suffer for you? Did any pocketbook go to the cross to save you?

Oh, accept God's plan and be saved. Believe! Believe! Don't plead your own righteousness. Were the sinner a thousand times better than all the claims of the self-righteousness, that would be no ground of hope. Were he ten thousand times guilty of all the works of the flesh—adultery, fornication, etc.—that need be no ground of despair. Don't be as those who refuse God's diamonds and accept the devil's dirt—nor as those who choose to leave God's highway for the devil's dead-end street.

"To him give all the prophets witness, that through his name, whosoever believeth in him shall receive remission of sins" (Acts 10: 43). ". . . through this man is preached unto you the forgiveness of sins: And by him all that believe are justified from all things, from which ye could not be justified by the law of Moses" (Acts 13:38–39).

In the matter of the sinner's acceptance with God, good works form no part whatsoever. If sinners were a thousand times better than they are, they could not be saved without coming to Christ. If sinners were ten thousand times more wretched and callous of heart and life than they are, coming to Christ with penitent and believing heart, they would straightway be received to the bosom and encircled in the arms of God's merciful and forgiving love.

And this brings us at last, to speak of:

9. THE PERIOD—"NOW":

All truth as to the brevity of life, all thoughts as to the length of eternity point to that word "Now." All belief as to the certainty and horror of hell—the place where "hell's infernal drums beat time to the ceaseless groans of the lost amid incessant and unmitigated and unquenchable torment"—points to the word "now." All descriptions that cause us to think of the heaven wherein the servants of Christ shall have an eternity of bliss in His glorified presence—in that place where there is no unhallowed ambition, no strife and no sin, where all hearts beat in unison, where all songs are songs of love, where the trees are trees of life, where there is fullness of joy and pleasures forevermore—yes, all such descriptions of heaven point urgently to the period of the *now*.

The great barrier of getting people saved is that they are not willing to be saved in God's *way* and *time*. God's way is Christ. God's time is *now*.

At what time shall we believe? The time to believe on the Son of God is now—not tomorrow, not some other time. There is not a word in God's book which tells us that any one is justified in putting off his belief for one day, one hour, one minute. "For he saith, I have heard thee in a time accepted, and in the day of salvation have I succoured thee: . . . behold, now is the day of salvation" (II Corinthians 6:2).

Business relations and affairs prove no man wise and justify no man in delaying to believe. "But seek ye first the kingdom of God and his righteousness; and all these things shall be added unto you" (Matthew 6:33).

Delay—really a decision for the wrong way—is unsafe. "Boast not thyself of tomorrow; for thou knowest not what a day may bring forth" (Proverbs 27:1).

God commands us to believe now. "Seek ye the Lord while he may be found, call ye upon him while he is near:" (Isaiah 55:6). "Be ye not as your fathers, unto whom the former prophets have cried, saying, Thus saith the Lord of hosts; Turn ye now from your evil ways, and from your evil doings: but they did not hear, nor hearken unto me, saith the Lord" (Zechariah 1:4).

Thus you are taught—and warned—that no one is warranted in putting off repentance and believing for a moment. Life is so brief— ". . . a vapour, that appeareth for a little time and then vanisheth away." (James 4:14)—a thin footprint upon a sea-lashed shore, the stay of a postman, a glimpse of a passing ship, a quick sob in the night, a burst of music down a crowded street. ". . . we spend our years as a tale that is told" (Psalms 90:9). "Swift to its close ebbs out life's little day." Time is not on your side. The shortness of our day is a truth we all know and forget. And Death, whose only music is the sob of broken hearts, whose only pleasure fountains are falling tears, is not on your side. When Death's leaden sceptre is laid on your cold bosom, no mistakes can be rectified any more—for as soon as the breath leaves the body the decree of an immutable God rolls over the shrouded form.

". . . Today if ye will hear his voice, harden not your hearts" (Hebrews 4:7). But so many say "tomorrow." Tomorrow is the philosophy of fools, the subterfuge of procrastinators, the day that never is. Tomorrow is a ship in which many have gone to shipwreck, a lamp that failed and left many in eternal darkness, a guillotine that has beheaded hopes of heaven, a key that has locked many in dungeons of despair, an inexorable jailor that has imprisoned many behind hell's bars. Tomorrow is the road that has often led to the House of Never.

> Tomorrow and tomorrow and tomorrow
> Creeps in this petty race from day to day,
> To the last syllable of recorded time;
> And all our yesterdays have lighted fools
> The way to dusty death.

"Whereas ye know not what shall be on the morrow. For what is your life? It is even a vapour, that appeareth for a little time, and then vanisheth away" (James 4:14).

Life is too short for us to be saying "Tomorrow." Wisdom disclaims the word, nor holds society with those who own it. We say again: ". . . now is the accepted time; behold, now is the day of salvation" (II Corinthians 6:2). And he that believeth on the Son hath —right *now*—everlasting life. Be not guilty of the most sinful sin of all sins—the rejection of Christ. We must either meet Christ bearing our sin, with all our sins upon us, or we must find someone else to bear our sins for us. If we should meet this holy God with our sin upon us then we must be forever banished from His presence—". . . be punished with everlasting destruction from the presence of the Lord, and from the glory of his power;" (II Thessalonians 1:9). But if you accept Him, no matter how long you have sinned, no matter how greatly you have sinned, you can meet God with absolutely no sin upon you. It is enough for you, if you had a million souls with a million sins against each of them—". . . the blood of Jesus Christ his Son cleanseth us from all sin" (I John 1:7). The greatest sinner in the world needs no more. The littlest sinner in the world can do with no less. God says "Now." Satan, the malicious enemy of your soul, says "Tomorrow." What do *you* say?

Believe now on the Son of God who came down from the heights of deity to the depths of humanity for you—down from the adorations of heaven to the abominations of earth, down from the corona-

tions of heaven to the curses of men, down from the glory place to
the gory place, down from heaven's joys to earth's hell-instigated jeers,
down from heaven's throne to the tree on Calvary's hill, down from
the worship of angels to the wrath of Christ-despising men.

Oh, for His sake and your soul's sake, settle this matter of salvation *now!* Or, if you are a backslider, return *now* unto Christ. Or, if
you are a Christian who is giving God hours when he asks for days,
finding all duties boresome, giving God only a tame half-heartedness
in service, you can now give Him first place in your life. Do it now!
Put aside your righteousness and accept Christ's—*now*. As a Christian put aside your do-littleness, or do-nothingness, and give Him
your best.

As the voice of conscience speaks, saying "Now," so does the voice
of the Spirit of God speak, saying "Believe on the Son of God now."
What mercy from God that you are still alive and under hope of
heavenly grace. Take refuge in Christ whose blood cleanseth from
all sin.

Death, whose relentless scythe mows down the rich and the poor,
may be near. Eternity may be at the door. Sinner, perhaps this very
day, your last accepted time may be on your doorstep. If again you
should drive the Spirit of God away, then hope may never again
beam on you. The day of grace being a short day, there is need of
haste. A free and full pardon is offered through faith in Christ and
His blood. Take it—and you will have peace with God. Prefer not
the world's rags, as polluted silks, to heaven's rich robes. Prefer not
Satan's paste pebbles to Christ's jewels. Prefer not the shadow to the
substance. Prefer not the body that shall be turned over to corruption
and the worm, to the soul with capacities for God.

I charge you, men and women, rest not until you have Him as
your precious Redeemer. If you die without Him, or if you are unsaved when He comes, you must be shut out of His bright presence
forever. Come to Him as he IS—and now. Come to Him as you are
—now! Come now and believe on Him and love Him and live for
Him until the pierced hands that opened to you the gates to grace
shall open to you the gates to glory.

II

Consequences of Man's Alliance with Satan

Now is the judgment of this world: now shall the prince of this world be cast out (John 12:31).
Hereafter I will not talk much with you: for the prince of this world cometh, and hath nothing in me (John 14:30).
Of judgment, because the prince of this world is judged (John 16:11).

---

1. The Tree-sign:

And out of the ground made the LORD God to grow every tree that is pleasant to the sight, and good for food; the tree of life also in the midst of the garden, and the tree of knowledge of good and evil (Genesis 2:9).

At Calvary—the abyss of the world's greatest sorrow, the summit of the world's highest hopes—God, in bloody garments dressed, courted sinful humanity's love. There stood a bloody tree whose roots reached into the councils of eternity. Peter, right after fear came upon all the church in Jerusalem, commanded by the hostile council not to teach in the name of Jesus, spoke of that tree: "The God of our fathers raised up Jesus, whom ye slew and hanged on a tree" (Acts 5:30).

Peter, right after refusing to be worshipped by Cornelius in the house of Cornelius, spoke again of that tree—telling how God anointed Jesus with the Holy Ghost and with power, telling how Jesus went about doing good and healing all who were oppressed of the devil, declaring that God was with Jesus, saying: "And we are witnesses of all things which he did both in the land of the Jews, and in Jerusalem; whom they slew and hanged on a tree:" (Acts 10:39).

Paul, who counted all things but loss that he might know Jesus and the power of His resurrection and the fellowship of His suffering (Philippians 3:10), spoke in the synagogue in Antioch of Pisidia of that tree whose blossoms were blood, saying: "And though they found no cause of death in him, yet desired they Pilate that he should be slain. And when they had fulfilled all that was written of him, they took him down from the tree, and laid him in a sepulchre" (Acts 13: 28–29).

And Paul, from whose pen Gospel truths fell like golden pollen from the stems of shaken lilies, wrote to the Galatians of that gory tree on which the Prince of life (Acts 3:15) and Prince of the kings of the earth (Revelation 1:5) died: "Christ hath redeemed us from the curse of the law, being made a curse for us: for it is written, Cursed is every one that hangeth on a tree:" (Galatians 3:13).

And Peter, whose pen was as mighty as his tongue was fiery, wrote: "Who his own self bare our sins in his own body on the tree, that we, being dead to sins, should live unto righteousness: by whose stripes ye were healed" (I Peter 2:24).

And the reason for this Calvary tree on which the second Adam, Jesus Christ, weltered in the flames of divine wrath for six awful hours till His heart burst and blood flowed out to the satisfaction of divine justice, is the tree of which Adam ate in Eden's garden. A far reach it is from the tree on Calvary's bleak hill across the stormy chasms of pre-crucifixion history to Eden's flowery garden. But they have very intimate relations—relations made before the pillars of the earth were placed in their sockets and before the first ray of light sped like some archangel with garments afire across the uncharted dark.

Traveling from the Calvary tree to the Eden tree, we pass along the street where Jesus Christ, in physical exhaustion, fell beneath the weight of that cross-shaped tree; and through Pilate's court where, with keen and merciless scourge, they tore His flesh to shreds as eagle beaks tear the flesh of turtle dove. And near that cross-shaped tree on a hill, like a skull, is Gethsemane's garden where the roots of

His divine emotion put forth their crimson tears. And we pass from that sacred garden to the upper room where, with His thoughts upon the tree, He changed wine into the perpetual symbol of His blood.

And on to the Mount of Transfiguration where, before the eyes of three amazed disciples, the spiritual incandescence of His deity burst through the veil of His flesh ". . . and his face did shine as the sun, and his raiment was white as the light" (Matthew 17:2).

And on to Lake Galilee where He, who later would conquer death, made the raging waves to lie like sleeping dogs at His feet and the winds howling like maniacs to whisper like babes breathing softly in sleep.

And on to Jordan where His burial in baptism foreshadowed the grim event, the center of which is Jesus who endured the cross and despised the shame thereof, in order that the captives of the Law might go free and the prison doors be opened to those who are bound.

And on to Nazareth where, by toil with the tools of men and by the sweat of His brow, He sanctified all honest labor.

And on to Bethlehem where, as Milton puts it, "that glorious form wherewith he wont at Heaven's high council table to sit the midst of Tribal Unity, he laid aside"—where, to use kindred words, He gathered up his pre-incarnate glory and shrouded it in the facts and purposes of the incarnation.

And on from Bethlehem, we make our flight across the four dumb centuries and on to Solomon's glorious and gold-covered Temple where all the blood on the Temple altars shed, pointed to Christ the heavenly Lamb who takes all our sins away—all sacrifices significant shadows of redemptive entity still ahead, adumbrations of a substance yet to come.

And on to the altar of the wilderness Tabernacle where lambs and bullocks brought to death by piercing knives pointed to Christ pierced with nails—the holy and propellent center to which the faith of mankind before and since gravitated.

And on to the blood-stained lintels of the Passover night which guaranteed deliverance to the first born, as the blood foreshadowed a deliverance for all mankind far greater through Christ whom Paul described as ". . . our Passover sacrificed for us:" (I Corinthians 5:7).

And on to Eden's garden where, at the tree of which the first Adam ate, Despair pitched his black pavillion upon the sterile and blasted fields of man's lost estate. Luther said: "The tree of the knowledge of good and evil has become Adam's altar and pulpit, from which he was to render due benevolence to God, recognize God's word and will and give thanks; and had Adam not fallen this tree would have been like a temple and cathedral." Looking at this tree, a sign of God's rule over man and the subjection of man to God, let that tree speak to us—even as Jesus said: ". . . learn a parable of the fig tree;" (Mark 13:28), and ". . . learn of me;" (Matthew 11:29). At this tree we learn that God who made man "in his own image, after his own likeness"—meaning that Adam was great, wise, holy—at this tree we learn that God, in kindness, put a restriction upon man, in wisdom; and in wisdom imposed upon the first Adam a limitation of liberty—the sign of which limitation is that tree in the midst of the garden.

> And the LORD God took the man, and put him into the garden of Eden to dress it and to keep it. And the LORD God commanded the man, saying, Of every tree of the garden thou mayest freely eat: But of the tree of the knowledge of good and evil, thou shalt not eat of it: for in the day that thou eatest thereof thou shalt surely die (Genesis 2:15-17).

Reading of this tree in the Bible, we learn that it was "the tree of the *knowledge* of good and evil." And I believe it was a literal tree—not an allegorical or mythical tree.

G. Campbell Morgan, speaking of Genesis three, said: "This is the story of actual events in physical life of a spiritual nature. Spiritual evil is here represented as taking physical form to reach spiritual man through his physical being. We must, therefore, consider the physical facts—always observing the spiritual value. We have travelled far from these primitive simplicities, but we have not travelled any distance from their essential meanings."

Says the erudite Moyer: "We believe that there was nothing sinful about the tree itself, and to eat of its fruit was not wrong in itself. The question here is not one of a tree, but one of obedience."

This tree God kept to Himself as a token of His sovereignty.

This tree God guarded with a restriction as a token of His absolute authority over man.

This tree was a *sign* of the rule of God over man and the subjection of man to God. But "even in the prohibition God wished far more to give than to withhold. The tree . . . had in a double manner a divine purpose; it was a means in the hand of God for the education of man and by this for the transfiguration of the earth." (Erich Sauer, in *The Dawn of World Redemption* [Wm. B. Erdmans].)

At this tree in Eden, man lost his Eden—his home and unmarred and indescribable happiness.

At this tree, sin entered Eden.

At this tree, the chaotic condition of the world today had its genesis.

At this tree, death entered the human race. "Wherefore, as by one man sin entered into the world, and death by sin; and so death passed upon all men, for that all have sinned:" (Romans 5:12).

At this tree in Paradise—this tree which was the sign of God's sovereignty and absolute authority over man, man's hell began.

Think of:

2. THE TEMPTER—SATAN: The only source of information is the one Book which discloses the fact of his personality, portrays his character, defines his origin and activity, and warns against his devices. The Scriptures unfold a detailed description of the person and career of Satan from his beginning, throughout the development of his kingdom, down to his final overthrow. The Bible does not argue to prove his existence and personality. But it does speak of him in terms that can only mean that he does exist and that he exists as a *person*. And the Bible presents him as a person so prominent and powerful in the world today that our hearts would fail us were it not for our faith in Christ and His power and wisdom.

This personality—Satan—is the being through whom sin was introduced into the human race.

Now the serpent was more subtil than any beast of the field which the
LORD God had made. And he said unto the woman, Yea, hath God
said, Ye shall not eat of every tree of the garden? And the woman
said unto the serpent, We may eat of the fruit of the trees of the garden: But of the fruit of the tree which is in the midst of the garden,
God hath said, Ye shall not eat of it, neither shall ye touch it, lest ye
die. And the serpent said unto the woman, Ye shall not surely die:
For God doth know that in the day ye eat thereof, then your eyes
shall be opened, and ye shall be as gods, knowing good and evil
(Genesis 3:1–5).

The serpent of Genesis three is not a snake but Satan himself. Do
you believe in the personality of the devil? Do you say, "No?" Do you
say that? Then you believe that everything dark and devilish and
damnable in human life has come out of human nature. It simply is
not true. Whatever has blasted human life did not originate in human
life, but with Satan—a mighty personality. In fifteen books of the
Bible, Satan is mentioned one hundred and seventeen times—and in
each case he is spoken of as a real personality.

"Now the serpent." Dr. G. Campbell Morgan says concerning
this: "It seems to me this is a somewhat unfortunate translation and
that it is not the essential meaning of the Hebrew word—*Nawchash*.
It is quite true the word is used for 'snake' but it has another signifi-
cation and is used in other applications. The word—*Nawchash*—
literally means a shining one."

And in the guise of a shining personality—bewildering and be-
dazzling Eve by the brilliance of his appearance—he beguiled Eve
(II Corinthians 11:3). In his subtlety, I believe that Satan—one of
the most beautiful, wonderful, intellectual, musical beings ever created—transformed himself into an angel of light (II Corinthians 11:
14) and made his interrogatory assault on Eve.

The devil was perfect in his creation. In Ezekiel 28, Satan is
described under the title of "The King of Tyrus." What is addressed
to "The King of Tyrus" is, by its character, seen to be a direct refer-
ence to the person of Satan. For no similar person to whom this
description could apply is revealed in the Scriptures. Every sentence

of this extended passage is a distinct revelation and is worthy of long and careful study. He was not always the devil; he *became* the devil. He did not always exist; he was created. God did not create the devil. He created the being who later became Satan; John 8:44 states that he ". . . abode not in the truth, . . ." He was once in the truth. He was created in the truth—but he abode not in it. "Thou wast perfect in thy ways from the day that thou wast created, till iniquity was found in thee" (Ezekiel 28:15). Satan as he came from God's hand was the most exalted of God's creatures. "Thou sealest up the sum." The sum of all created perfection. There could be nothing added to him. He was "full of wisdom." He was "perfect in beauty."

The Devil is a created being. He is therefore not self-existent. Nor eternal. But limited and finite. His creation was after the order of the angels. The angels were not the off-spring of a family relation. Cradlehood and all the tender ties, training, and growth are unknown to them. Each angel is created—not born. Created directly, personally by God. The Devil was created good—perfect in beauty. His purity, as well as exaltation, were sources of congratulation, wonderment and praise in heaven. Speaking by the mouth of Ezekiel, the Lord says he was created perfect in all his ways—full of wisdom, perfect in beauty, and next to God, supreme in power. God made him perfect and clean—he made himself Satan. God gave him liberty, glory, power. He made himself the Devil. This answers the question: "Why did God make the Devil?" He never made one. He became the Devil by his own act. He rebelled against God.

> How art thou fallen from heaven, O Lucifer, son of the morning! how art thou cut down to the ground, which didst weaken the nations! For thou hast said in thine heart, I will ascend into heaven, I will exalt my throne above the stars of God: I will sit also upon the mount of the congregation, in the sides of the north: I will ascend above the heights of the clouds; I will be like the most High. Yet thou shalt be brought down to hell, to the sides of the pit (Isaiah 14: 12–15).

Satan was the first being to manifest a will opposed to the will of God. "I will ascend into heaven" shows that he was at the time

ruling beneath heaven. "I will ascend above the clouds" shows that
he was on earth. "I will ascend above the stars of God" shows his
jealousy of Jesus. "I will become like the most High" shows his ego-
tism and ambition. "Thou shalt be brought down to hell" shows,
or foretells his doom.

> Thine heart was lifted up because of thy beauty, thou hast corrupted
> thy wisdom by reason of thy brightness: I will cast thee to the ground,
> I will lay thee before kings, that they may behold thee (Ezekiel 28:
> 17).

And this Satan, the Devil, was a most real and grim person to Jesus
Christ. Jesus recognized his person. Jesus felt and acknowledged his
power. Jesus abhorred his character. Jesus warred against his personal
kingdom. Jesus designated him the prince of the world: "Now is the
judgment of this world: now shall the prince of this world be cast
out" (John 12:31). "Hereafter I will not talk much with you: for the
prince of this world cometh, and hath nothing in me" (John 14:30).
"Of judgment, because the prince of this world is judged" (John 16:
11).

James spoke of him as a person: "Submit yourselves therefore to
God. Resist the devil, . . ." (James 4:7).

Peter spoke of him as a person: "Be sober, be vigilant; because
your adversary the devil, as a roaring lion, walketh about, seeking
whom he may devour" (I Peter 5:8). Paul spoke of him as a person:
"And that they may recover themselves out of the snare of the devil,
who are taken captive by him at his will" (II Timothy 2:26). "And no
marvel; for Satan himself is transformed into an angel of light" (II
Corinthians 11:14).

John spoke of him as a person: "And the great dragon was cast
out, that old serpent, called the Devil, and Satan, which deceiveth
the whole world: he was cast out into the earth, and his angels were
cast out with him" (Revelation 12:9).

Satan is the embodiment of evil in a person. Not only personality
is attributed to him, but fatherhood likewise. He is the father of all

evil—ever the enemy of Jesus and ever malignant, active, crafty, cautious, cowardly.

Through this Tempter came:

3. THE TRANSGRESSION—SIN: In the Edenic paradise where God united heaven and earth, sin entered.

> And when the woman saw that the tree was good for food, and that it was pleasant to the eyes, and a tree to be desired to make one wise, she took of the fruit thereof, and did eat, and gave also unto her husband with her; and he did eat (Genesis 3:6).

Thus sin, black as night, drove the morning splendor of Eden out, and henceforth the earth stood under the shadow of death. In disobedience to God man denied the sovereignty of God and pushed God from the throne of his heart. Sin—mutiny and revolt against God —caused rebellion of the individual will of the creature against God's universal order.

Sin—the power that reversed man's nature, destroyed the harmony of his powers, threw him woefully deranged, miserable, ungoverned, erratic, lost, into interminable leagues of night.

Sin—the evil that subverted the constitutional order of his nature dismantled him of his nobility, brought him in unconditional surrender to diabolical power, caused him treacherously to give up the keys of the soul's citadel placed in his keeping.

Eve—the first woman, the first wife, the first mother,—was first in this awful transgression. "And Adam was not deceived, but the woman being deceived was in the transgression" (I Timothy 2:14). Adam's identification with the sin of his wife brought sin into this world. "Wherefore, as by one man sin entered into the world, and death by sin; and so death passed upon all men, for that all have sinned:" (Romans 5:12).

Because of sin, whose only flowers grow among skulls and have no perfume, every stream with human crime is stained, every breeze with moral miasma corrupted, every day's light blackened, every life's cup tainted with the bitter, every life's roadway made dangerous

with pitfalls, every life's voyage made perilous with treacherous
shoals.

Though some foolishly assert that to eat of a forbidden fruit
was no more than nibbling a dainty, "no more than tasting an apple,"
just testing the flavour of the fruit, they see not that it was the sinful
seeking on the part of the primal pair to rise to equal exaltation with
God (Genesis 3:5). So many believe not that Adam's sin was a crime
of the greatest enormity.

With a mind illuminated by the Holy Spirit, Adam showed gross
infidelity—believing Satan rather than God. Adam, the recipient and
beneficiary of everything that was necessary for the perfection and
perpetration of his happiness, was guilty of discontent and envy in
thinking God had denied him something necessary to his happiness.
In the very presence of God, it was prodigious pride in showing desire to be like God. Fortified sufficiently to resist temptation, he was
guilty of sacrilegious theft in purloining what God had reserved for
himself as token of his sovereignty. And without compulsion, he
committed suicide and murder—in bringing death upon himself and
all his posterity. Adam brought on himself and all succeeding ages
the wretched results of sin and death. There was but a single point at
which Adam could revolt against God. Environed as he was, the
awful social sins that have cancered the race could make no appeal
to him. He had no occasion to bow down before another God—because God was his counsellor and friend, and there were no other
gods. There was no provocation that could tempt him to take God's
name in vain. There was no Sabbath to break—because all days were
holy. He had no father or mother to dishonor. There was no fellow
man to cheat in a business transaction. To commit murder was un-
thinkable. The Seventh Commandment, had it been written then,
would have meant nothing to the man whose wife was "in the image
of God"—and the only woman on earth. Stealing was impossible—
because all things belonged to him. False witness and covetousness
against a neighbor could not be—he had no neighbor. But when God
selected for Himself a single tree as a token of His sovereignty and
of man's submission to that sovereignty, Adam, in rebellion, would

not abide content that God should be over and above him—and that sets forth the crux of every contention between the Divine and the human.

Adam's act of rebellion introduced the leaven of moral disintegration into the harmonious family of worlds and systems of worlds. His revolt against God's sovereignty was an act spurning the dignity of his own endowment—a casting from his brow the crown of his lordship. Adam's transgression was not "just biting into forbidden fruit," but an act involving a countless host of unborn creatures in unmeasured misery. Moreover, an act so pregnant with all evil could not fail to pass in review before the eye of Infinite Holiness and Divine Justice—because Law without penalty is only advice. The penalty of sin must be consonant with the dignity, power, glory, honor, holiness, justice, and truth of him against whom the offense is committed.

> And unto Adam he said, Because thou hast hearkened unto the voice of thy wife, and hast eaten of the tree, of which I commanded thee, saying, Thou shalt not eat of it; cursed is the ground for thy sake; in sorrow shalt thou eat of it all the days of thy life; Thorns also and thistles shall it bring forth to thee; and thou shalt eat the herb of the field; in the sweat of thy face shalt thou eat bread, till thou return unto the ground; for out of it wast thou taken: for dust thou art, and unto dust shalt thou return (Genesis 3:17–19).

That gives us—because of man's sin—the curse upon the earth and the judgment upon man. From such award by the Righteous Judge, there is no appeal. One look at the experience of the race over a period of thousands of years teaches us that the judgment took effect. Shocked then to its core and center, creation has trembled ever since. Living as we are in a fallen world, we see that no island of all the seas and no continent of earth has escaped. As the material earth utters its groan and its protest, so the material and physical sufferings that have characterized all generations testify to the legacy of woe transmitted by Adam's transgression to all generations. God hath joined guilt and punishment—and what God hath joined let none attempt to put asunder.

Let us give thought now to:

4. THE TURPITUDE—THE SHAME: By that I mean the world's shameless wickedness evidenced by man's obedience to and co-operation with Satan. We do not have to be photographers of sordid spots or drivers of garbage wagons to know that ". . . all the world may become guilty before God" (Romans 3:19)—that new troops of malignant fevers come from the lungs of the world, that corruption inhabits the blood of the world, and that millions "loose wild tongues that hold not God in awe."

John, the Apostle, described the world today when he said: "And we know . . . the whole world lieth in wickedness" (I John 5:19). Something of the sad situation is glimpsed in Winston Churchill's words: "I do not intend to preside over the dissolution of the British Empire." And it is glimpsed by others—by Judge Hunt of Los Angeles: "Traitors betray us at every opportunity." By Chief Justice Earl Warren: "In a world of international gangsterism, oppression and unbelief, nothing is more necessary than a resurgence of Christian faith." By the late U.S. Senator Charles Tobey: "The trouble is that America today has a lack of Christian stamina." By Whitaker Chambers: "History is cluttered with the wreck of nations that became indifferent to God—and died."

Satan is active. At present he is ". . . the prince of the power of the air, the spirit that now worketh in the children of disobedience:" (Ephesians 2:2). And on earth, he ". . . your adversary the devil, as a roaring lion, walketh about, seeking whom he may devour" (I Peter 5:8). He is also ". . . the god of this world . . ." (II Corinthians 4:4), this present world-system, this present social order, which he has organized upon the principles of self-will, self-interest, self-seeking, sinful pleasure, socialism, humanism, and all other devices to blind men to the rights and claims of God to their sole devotion and obedience. He could not become God, he can never become God, so during this age he has become "the ape of God." Paul's recognition of this fact is indicated by his warning: "Put on the whole armour of God, that ye may be able to stand against the wiles of the devil. For we wrestle not against flesh and blood, but against principalities, against powers, against the rulers of the darkness of this world, against the spiritual wickedness in high places" (Ephesians 6:11-12).

Satan is a murderer. "Ye are of your father the devil, and the lusts of your father ye will do. He was a murderer from the beginning, and abode not in the truth, because there is no truth in him. When he speaketh a lie, he speaketh of his own: for he is a liar, and the father of it" (John 8:44). Satan is a liar. And he is such a liar that he can not tell the truth without lying. The terror of the story of Eden, as to Satan's part, is that in every word of Satan there is an element of truth.

Satan is a sinner. "He that committeth sin is of the devil; for the devil sinneth from the beginning. For this purpose the Son of God was manifested, that he might destroy the works of the devil" (I John 3:8).

Satan is an adversary and devourer. "Be sober, be vigilant; because your adversary the devil, as a roaring lion, walketh about, seeking whom he may devour" (I Peter 5:8).

Satan is an *enemy*. "But while men slept, his enemy came and sowed tares among the wheat, and went his way. . . . The enemy that sowed them is the devil; the harvest is the end of the world; and the reapers are the angels" (Matthew 13:25, 39).

Satan is an *accuser*. "And I heard a loud voice saying in heaven, Now is come salvation, and strength, and the kingdom of our God, and the power of his Christ: for the accuser of our brethren is cast down, which accused them before our God day and night" (Revelation 12:10).

Satan is a *tempter*. "Then was Jesus led up of the Spirit into the wilderness to be tempted of the devil. And when he had fasted forty days and forty nights, he was afterward an hungered. And when the tempter came to him, he said, If thou be the Son of God, command that these stones be made bread" (Matthew 4:1-3). "For this cause, when I could no longer forbear, I sent to know your faith, lest by some means the tempter have tempted you, and our labour be in vain" (I Thessalonians 3:5).

And this enemy of all good, and mighty adversary of God—

called Dragon, old Serpent, Devil, Satan—has "the wherewithall and the whomwithall" to wreak havoc in the world. To help him in his work against God and man he has:

Angels: ". . . Depart from me, ye cursed, into everlasting fire, prepared for the devil and his angels:"—Matthew 25:41.

Messengers: "And lest I should be exalted above measure through the abundance of the revelations, there was given to me a thorn in the flesh, a messenger of Satan to buffet me, lest I should be exalted above measure" (II Corinthians 12:7).

Ministers: ". . . for Satan himself is transformed into an angel of light. Therefore it is no great thing if his ministers also be transformed as the ministers of righteousness; whose end shall be according to their works" (II Corinthians 11:14, 15).

Followers: "For some are already turned aside after Satan" (I Timothy 5:15).

Children: ". . . the children of the devil . . ." (I John 3:10). "Ye are of your father the devil . . ." (John 8:44).

Works: ". . . For this purpose the Son of God was manifested, that he might destroy the works of the devil" (I John 3:8).

Snares: ". . . the snare of the devil" (I Timothy 3:7). ". . . that they may recover themselves out of the snare of the devil, who are taken captive by him at his will" (II Timothy 2:26).

Wiles: "Put on the whole armour of God, that ye may be able to stand against the wiles of the devil" (Ephesians 6:11).

Devices: "Lest Satan should get an advantage of us: for we are not ignorant of his devices" (II Corinthians 2:11).

Power: ". . . to turn from darkness to light, and from the power of Satan unto God, . . ." (Acts 26:18). Also ". . . whose coming is after the working of Satan with all power . . ." (II Thessalonians 2:9).

Wrath: ". . . Woe to the inhabiters of the earth and of the sea! For the devil is come down to you, having great wrath, because he knoweth that he hath but a short time" (Revelation 12:12).

A Will: ". . . taken captive by him at his will" (II Timothy 2:26).

It is little wonder, then, that Satan—the old Serpent, the Dragon, the Devil, since he has angels and messengers and ministers and followers and children and works and snares and wiles and devices and power and wrath, who wields such power over man, in getting man to obey him and disobey God—is he who has, because of his power over men, brought about the whole evil state of the world.

That truth no doubt was glimpsed by Walter Lippman when he wrote: "No mariner has ever entered upon a more uncharted sea than the human being born in our Today. Never were roads wilder, nor sign posts fewer. Our ancestors knew their way from birth through death into eternity, but we are puzzled about day after tomorrow."

Maybe that is why W. B. Siff wrote in *Two Worlds*: "A world-wide neurosis and morbid disregard for old values mark the spiritual unhingement of multitudes of men."

Maybe, too, Cordell Hull, some years ago, knew something of Satan's work when he wrote: "The specter of a new descent into the conditions of international anarchy which characterized the Dark Ages looms on the horizon of today. I am profoundly convinced that it menaces the civilized existence of mankind."

And Sumner Welles, speaking before the meeting of the Foreign Policy Association in New York, said: "We are living in a rotten world." Dorothy Thompson, noted world observer, wrote: "We are in a new Dark Ages. Civilization has already capitulated to barbarism by default of its own standards."

Gov. Saltonstall of Massachusetts: "In the last generation we have watched the moral and spiritual life of the whole world deteriorate to a marked degree."

President Eisenhower: "Unless we have a moral and spiritual regeneration, we shall all go up in a cloud of atomic dust." Satan's power over unbelieving mankind made possible such a statement.

H. G. Wells: "The Red flag will advance to the Rhine and from the Rhine to the Atlantic—and anarchy will seize these doomed United States of America." Man's obedience to Satan has hung just such a black pall over America.

Today, people who by wisdom know not God and who are administrators of laughing gas for the painless extraction of sin, no longer believe that ". . . the wrath of God is revealed from heaven against all ungodliness and unrighteousness of men, who hold the truth in unrighteousness" (Romans 1:18).

Today we have a world weary with new tracks of thought, with lust, and ripe for destruction. Everywhere we look we are faced by upheaval, war, revolution, failure. Monarchy and republicanism, dictatorship and democracy have failed. We are faced by national and international bankruptcy. This is a day of daring defiance, when by supercilious pose, by an attitude of intellectual superiority and by a critical and skeptical attitude toward the supernatural, there is a substitution of out-worn, man-made philosophies and pseudo-science for the living Word of God's revelation—a parroting of the skepticism of free-thinkers.

Today, Satan's power over unbelieving millions in the world has sent men out to war's bloody butchery to build a fence of skulls and skeletons around the world.

Today, you get evidence of man's obedience to Satan and of man's accepting his carousel when you behold the corporate sin and the anarchy among the nations of the world.

Think of our unreasonable devotion to sensual satisfactions, of our insane scrambles after gain, of the unmitigated villainies of multitudes. Think of our undisciplined liberalism that goes nowhere so fast it arrives out of breath, talking more and more of less and less. The Bible is summoned to appear at the bar of human reason. Spiritual mercury falls low. Faith's wings are clipped by reason's scissors.

Look at Korea! What but man's obedience to Satan has caused so much blood to soak the soil on Heartbreak Ridge and Sniper's Point? Think of the disease-ridden multitudes of war-ravaged Europe—to whom a crust would be a banquet and the scrapings of our garbage cans desirable—to whom our cast-off clothes would be as regal robes! Who but Satan and man's obedience to Satan could have lit the fires of such an awful conflagration? What but man's obedience to Satan could make mighty in the world this monstrous Communism—now exalting itself against God and eating, like a combination of dread diseases, at the vitals of our civilization. No wonder somebody said: "Cocktail politics cannot meet the challenge of this Goliath." Who, standing upon the Scriptural revelations and assertions, can say that the iron curtain and bamboo curtains are not devices of Satan to hold captive most of the world?

Today, Philistines of transcendent cleverness submit the warm wonder of Christianity to cool and merciless analysis and attack. Evils abound that would lead our greatest graces to the grave and leave no copy. Many ask us to substitute for Christianity's vital bread a chunk of cloud bank buttered with the night wind. This is a day of invertebrate theology, of jelly-fish morality, of India-rubber convictions, of see-saw religion, of somersault philosophy. There are spiritual latitudes as wide as the Sahara Desert and correspondingly dry. Civilization seems to be undergoing the frightful process of self-burial.

Moreover, we have today a menace of modernism which mutilates the Bible, minimizes sin, deifies man, and humanizes God.

But there shall come:

5. THE TERMINUS—SURENESS:

In our world there is the spirit of anti-Christ in continuing potency and pernicious prevalence. Of course, in this world of travail and pain this spirit of the anti-Christ will be dominant until it emerges in the person of the anti-Christ. ". . . anti-christ shall come . . ." (I John 2:18). That is the inspired pronouncement.

Little children, it is the last time: and as ye have heard that antichrist shall come, even now are there many anti-christs; whereby we know that it is the last time (I John 2:18).

And ". . . the Scripture cannot be broken;" (John 10:35). But the superman, with whom all the world will have to deal, will soon be here. Until he is here—exalting himself to the position of God (Daniel 11), speaking great words against the Most High and wearing out the saints of God (Daniel 7)—the spirit of this anti-Christ and apostasy will be ruinously rampant and destructively dominant.

Who is a liar but he that denieth that Jesus is the Christ? He is antichrist, that denieth the Father and the Son (I John 2:22).

For many deceivers are entered into the world, who confess not that Jesus Christ is come in the flesh. This is a deceiver and an antichrist (II John 7).

Of course, the culmination of the final world of anti-Christ now in the making is terrible tribulation involving the whole world. We read:

For then shall be great tribulation, such as was not since the beginning of the world to this time, no, nor ever shall be. And except those days should be shortened, there should be no flesh be saved: but for the elect's sake those days shall be shortened (Matthew 24:21–22).

Because thou hast kept the word of my patience, I also will keep thee from the hour of temptation, which shall come upon all the world, to try them that dwell upon the earth (Revelation 3:10).

In a day when some "choose the livery of heaven to serve the devil," there are those who substitute for Christ the God, Jesus the ethical teacher; substitute for His virgin birth, natural generation for Joseph; substitute for His miracles, mental manipulation; substitute for His shed blood, the spirit of self-sacrifice; substitute His resurrection from the grave, part-human influence; substitute for His "sure word of prophecy," twentieth century philosophy; substitute for His blood-bought church, a federation of Christendom.

And some today—in a land where Tom Paine could occupy some professedly Christian pulpits and be called Rev. Thomas Paine, D.D. —who distrust the deity of Christ and deride the efficacy of his blood are doing nothing short of spitting in the face of the God whose breath made the Book possible. These liberals—sounding their conjectural cornets and faith-flaunting flutes—speed along the highways and out into the bypaths of our educational, literary, scientific and theological highways, happily honking their horns, hogging the road and disregarding all the guide signs of ". . . the faith which was once delivered unto the saints" (Jude 3).

These coaxing conjecturers lay hold upon human minds and hearts as cancer smites the citadel of the human body or as tuberculosis blasts the delicate tissues of the lungs. Our intellectual atmosphere is oft unhealthy, our psychology is frequently destructive, our philosophy is oftentimes superficial and immoral, and the faith of our fathers is made a buffoon's bauble.

The inapprehensible bewitchment and the incogitable conclusions of the conjectural cauldron of these antisupernatural and anti-biblical wizards bring to mind what the second witch said in Act IV, Scene I of *Macbeth*:

> Fillet of a fenny snake,
> In the cauldron boil and bake;
> Eye of newt, and toe of frog,
> Wool of bat, and tongue of dog,
> Adder's fork, and blind-worm's sting,
> Lizard's leg, and owlet's wing,
> For a charm of powerful trouble,
> Like a hell-broth boil and bubble.

But in no assertions are they more false to the teaching of the Word of God than when they deny that the slaves of Satan and all who do his will have as their terminus, their end, an eternity with the devil in the lake of fire where "hell's infernal drums roll the eternal bars in hell's uproar, beating time to the ceaseless groans of the lost—amid incessant, unmitigated, unquenchable torment." Then, too, some sometimes scoff at the truth that the servants of Christ shall have as their terminus an eternity of bliss in the glorified presence of their Master whose pierced hands first opened to them the gates to grace, and then the gates to glory.

There are those who say that "hellfire is a riot of imaginative genius," a frightful dogma adding to the horrors and sorrows of the world," "a flagrant contradiction to the goodness of God," "in preaching an unauthorized accretion to the true doctrine," "in thinking the wild nightmare of a disordered brain." Some, basking in the light of academic lustre, declare the shallowness of their minds when they say that belief in heaven—terminus of all our earthly travels—is "the feeblest form of sickly sentimentality." But wise are Watkinson's words: "To take away hell is to reject the physician and leave the plague, to overthrow the lighthouse and leave the hidden rock, to wipe out the rainbow and leave the storm, to take away the vaccine and leave the smallpox."

And wise are all who believe and teach and preach concerning heaven—the place where no toil fatigues, no hostilities overcome, no temptations assail, no pain pierces, no sickness prostrates, no hand-to-hand fight for bread, no hearse rolls its way to the dark tomb. Heaven, where we see the wonders of the answer God gave to the prayer of Jesus: "Father, I will that they also, whom thou hast given me, be with me where I am; that they may behold my glory, which thou hast given me: for thou lovedst me before the foundation of the world" (John 17:24). Heaven—where there shall be no closed door in that glory to hide the Saviour from his blood-bought saints.

> Close to his trusted side
>   In fellowship divine,
> No cloud, no distance then shall hide
>   The glories great that there shall shine.

Soberly and with heart-searching and with proper evaluation of our resources and with faith that "we never test the resources of God until we attempt the impossible," we must, in view of all these things we have mentioned, consider:

6. THE TASK—SERVICE: Our task it is—as Christians. Our task it is to preach the Gospel—the Gospel as we find it defined by Paul in the words:

> Moreover, brethren, I declare unto you the gospel which I preached unto you. . . . For I delivered unto you first of all that which I also received, how that Christ died for our sins according to the scriptures; And that he was buried, and that he rose again the third day according to the scriptures: (I Corinthians 15:1-4).

That is our task—to preach the Gospel with all that means of the atoning death, of God manifest in the flesh, of the deity of the re-demptively-dying Christ as the only foundation of a reasonable faith. We are to preach the Gospel with all that means of his being cut off out of the land of the living as he made his grave with the wicked and with the rich in his death (Isaiah 53:8-9).

Yes, in our own land,—where there is much education that is godless and materialistic; Science, without intending to do so, has become the perverted apostle of savagery; Apostasy lifts its hydra-head in many places, and many, busy with cap and bells, with drink and dance, are talking nonsense on the edges of abysses—we must preach the truth that the virgin-born Christ was God incarnate, that the God incarnate was crucified, that this crucified One was buried, that the buried One rose bodily from the grave as the first sheaf of the resurrection harvest.

We must preach Christ's ascension and intercession and glorious return in a world where black snow falls, where the fever of life's fierce heat burns the divine dew off the grass, where spiritual mercury falls low, where faith's wings are clipped by reason's scissors, where fat deformities would compel us (if they could) to substitute for Christianity's vital bread a chunk of cloud bank buttered with the night wind, where our unregenerate humanity is set down in the midst of art, philosophies, and scientific wonders but remains a bedraggled beggar still—while many Christians are frost-bitten in realms of pleasure and idleness and luxury.

Christ crucified we must preach, knowing that His cross was a goal in the heart of God from all eternity, not a device God used to extricate himself from an emergency unforeseen by divine omniscience—the cross whereupon Christ, delivered by the determinate counsel and foreknowledge of God, was by wicked hands crucified and slain (Acts 2:23). The Gospel—with the atoning death and burial and resurrection of the incarnate God and His promised return—we must preach.

Preach it, not submit it for subdued discussion in the academic grove.

Preach it, not with piping voice, but with trumpet tones.

Preach it! Not as epicures in philosophy. Not as feeders of inflamed popular appetite for amusement. Not as administrators of laughing gas for the painless extraction of sin. Not as dainty tasters of intellectual subtleties. Not as experts in speculative cleverness dealing in the airy abstractions of an "up-to-date gospel." Not as dealers in fine-spun metaphysical disquisitions. But with a wooing urgency that lifts up the crucified Christ and warns men that the "... wrath of God is revealed from heaven against all ungodliness and unrighteousness of men, who hold the truth in unrighteousness;" (Romans 1:18).

Only thus shall we hope for any success in evangelizing our communities, our cities, and the world. We are to evangelize them, not Christianize them.

We are not to preach, believing we shall Christianize the world. We are not to send missionaries, believing they will Christianize Africa, China, Japan.

We are not to pray for evangelists, hoping they will save all America or Christianize England, France, or any other land. The Scripture says:

> Simeon hath declared how God at the first did visit the Gentiles, to take out of them a people for his name. And to this agree the words of the prophets; as it is written, After this I will return, and will build again the tabernacle of David, which is fallen down; and I will build again the ruins thereof, and I will set it up: (Acts 15:14–16).

That shows us God's plan and design. "God at the first did visit the Gentiles." To Christianize them? No. For what, then? To take out from among them "a people for his name." Then He will return.

In a world where there are more heathen than in the days of Jesus, more than at the close of the apostolic age, more than there were in the days of Carey and Judson, our task is *not* to Christianize the world. In a world where more heathen babies are being born in heathen homes than there are Christian converts being made in heathen lands, it is not the business of our churches and missionary agencies to *Christianize* the world, society, the nations, the social order, and to bring the principles of Jesus to bear upon politics. *Our task is to evangelize the world—to give every man a chance to accept Jesus Christ and be saved.*

When that has been done, the world has been evangelized. So let us keep to our God-given plan—keeping true to the vision of the Bible—and *evangelizing* the nations.

Lastly, let us consider:

7. THE TRIUMPH—SONG: In this world, how glorious it is to know that Christ and his followers have been used to bring light for those in darkness, liberty for those in bondage—breaking the chains of Satan for multitudes. "Forasmuch then as the children are partakers of flesh and blood, he also himself likewise took part of the same; that through death he might destroy him that had the power of death, that is, the devil;" (Hebrews 2:14). In Christ at last will mankind attain its blessed goal. He who appeared on earth and completed His work, humbled Himself from the heights of deity to the depths of humanity by going to the cross and bearing the sins of mankind,—He has ascended to heaven and now sits at the Father's right hand from whence He shall return and usher in the day on which He will present to Himself and to the Father His own people glorified (Ephesians 5:27).

He will triumph in that He will usher into the universe the day when life's current will flow back along its ancient channel and water all the Paradise regained, when the new heavens and the new earth will become the dwelling place of righteousness and consequent peace, when God's will shall be done in this new earth as it is now done in heaven.

Though the spirit of anti-Christ be mighty and subtle, though the person of anti-Christ be the devil's messiah, though lawlessness take the upper hand and the love of many grow cold (Matthew 24:12), though, when the Son of Man comes, He will find but *little* faith on the earth (Luke 18:8), though the increasing enmity of the world assures the expulsion of Christianity by civilization, still it is not a defeated but a triumphant Christ whom we love—a triumphant Christ who acknowledges no mastery in hostile circumstances.

Let no man deceive you by any means: for that day shall not come, except there come a falling away first, and that man of sin be revealed, the son of perdition; Who opposeth and exalteth himself above all that is called God, or that is worshipped; so that he as God sitteth in the temple of God, shewing himself that he is God.

And then shall that Wicked be revealed, whom the Lord shall consume with the spirit of his mouth, and shall destroy with the brightness of his coming: (II Thessalonians 2:3-4, 8).

The shattering of the kingdom of the world by the kingdom of God (Daniel 2:34-35 and Revelation 19:11-21)—this is the manner by which the affairs of the Lord will triumph after world-wide collapse and catastrophe; the stormers of heaven will be thrust down by heaven (Genesis 11:4).

Though the anti-Christ, as a false god, shall stand forth as the enemy of the true God and will demand for himself divine worship (II Thessalonians 2:3-4), though the coming of this idolatrous human abomination is ". . . after the working of Satan with all power and signs and lying wonders, . . ." (II Thessalonians 2:9), it shall be the Christ, to whom all power and authority in heaven and earth is given, who shall be victorious and triumphant. The devil and all his henchmen, the anti-Christ and all his forces, shall be defeated and destroyed and cast out from the presence of God and from before the face of man forever. Christ will get unto Himself a glorious victory, and in the "new heavens and the new earth" righteousness alone will reign forever and ever.

Since God is supreme, it must necessarily follow that He will compel all apparently contradictory conditions and conflicting circumstances to contribute to His causes. All apparently adverse plans and powers will be used to perfect His plans. This is what the Bible teaches—and whether we go to Paul, the prophet or the psalmist, we find affirmations of this truth. Paul said that God ". . . worketh all things after the counsel of his own will:" (Ephesians 1:11), while the psalmist says: "Surely the wrath of man shall praise thee: the remainder of wrath shalt thou restrain" (Psalms 76:10).

'Tis Christ who says: "To him that overcometh will I grant to sit with me in my throne, even as I also overcome, and am set down with my Father in his throne" (Revelation 3:21).

Until the pierced hands that opened to us the gates to grace shall open to us the gates to glory at His return—or at Death, if we be not among the living who shall be caught up to meet the Lord in the air —let us remember that the burden of Christ's message to the world is that there is life in Himself, and in Him alone—that He only is heaven's bread for earth's hunger and heaven's light for earth's darkness. Let us believe and preach and teach that He is the only fountain whence flow the waters of life—that He is the only Tree of Life whose leaves are for medicine and whose fruits are meat for the sick and starving millions of earth. He only will by the church make known to the principalities and powers in the heavenly places the manifold wisdom of God (Ephesians 3:10),—bringing out of all the earth's wild discord incomprehensible harmony ". . . according to the working whereby he is able even to subdue all things unto himself" (Philippians 3:21). This Christ "In whom are hid all the treasures of wisdom and knowledge" (Colossians 2:3), to us to whom is given the great and vast message to a lost and hopeless race—to us He promised success to the enterprise by pledging His wisdom to guide, His power to protect, His spirit to animate—timing and subordinating all opposition to the furtherance of his wise and gracious designs. Then, having led captivity captive, this triumphant Christ ascended on high to prepare a place for the spoils of His assured victory and triumph.

III

JUSTIFICATION

I know it is so of a truth: but how should man be just with God? (Job 9:2).
How then can man be justified with God? or how can he be clean that is born of a woman? (Job 25:4).

Job, who asked God questions through lips that festered with disease, yet trusting in God in the midst of his affliction, asked the above question twice.

The Apostle Paul, who compassed the earth with the truths of redemption, who counted all things but loss that he might know Jesus ". . . and the power of his resurrection, and the fellowship of his sufferings . . ." (Philippians 3:10), and who left a trail of Gospel glory across the Gentile world, answered Job by saying:

Therefore by the deeds of the law there shall no flesh be justified in his sight: for by the law is the knowledge of sin. But now the righteousness of God without the law is manifested, being witnessed by the law and the prophets; Even the righteousness of God which is by faith of Jesus Christ *unto* all and *upon* all them that believe: for there is no difference: For all have sinned, and come short of the glory of God; being justified freely by his grace through the redemption that is in Christ Jesus: whom God hath set forth to be a propitiation through faith in his blood, to declare his righteousness for the remission of sins that are past, through the forbearance of God; to declare, I say, at this time his righteousness: that he might be just, and the justifier of him which believeth in Jesus (Romans 3:20–26).

The Book of Romans, in which Paul's answer to Job is found, is a marvelous book indeed. Chrysostom had it read to him once each week. Melanchthon copied it twice with his own hand, in order to become better acquainted with it. Luther called it the chief book of the New Testament, and the perfect gospel. Coleridge regarded it as the profoundest book in existence. Sir William Ramsay referred to it as the philosophy of history. Godet spoke of it as the cathedral of Christian faith. Dr. David Bacon said that the faith of Christendom in its best periods has been more indebted to this epistle than to any other portion of the Living Oracles. Dr. W. H. Griffith Thomas asserted that a thorough study of Romans is a theological education in itself.

In this Book of Romans, as in all other books of the Bible, and as in all of life, we face:

1. THE TRAGEDY OF SIN, OR UNIVERSAL GUILT: The Spirit-guided Paul, in one of the most awful sentences he ever penned, declared that ". . . all the world may become guilty before God" (Romans 3:19).

David once moaned: "Have mercy upon me, O God, according to thy lovingkindness: according to the multitude of thy tender mercies blot out my transgressions" (Psalms 51:1). Thus he voiced the need of Palestine one thousand years before Jesus was born.

Judas—as one devil-ridden and conscience-scourged—spectacularly flung down the bloody coin in the court of the priest's hall and remorsefully sobbed: "I have sinned." Thus he voiced the *experience* of Palestine at the time of Christ.

The publican, as Jesus portrays him, stood up in the temple with guilty heart, and cried: "God be merciful to me a sinner." Thus he voiced the soul of all the ages since sin undermined the constitutional order of man's nature in Eden's garden. Guilty before God are all men!

And this sin of man is the heart-break of God.

For what the law could not do, in that it was weak through the flesh, God sending his own Son in the likeness of sinful flesh, and for sin, condemned sin in the flesh: (Romans 8:3).

Jesus did not *begin* to be the Man of Sorrows when He came down from the heights of deity to the depths of humanity and ministered as the Son of Man.

Jesus did not *cease* to be the Man of Sorrows when, marred and scarred with the stigmata of the cross, with the clouds as his chariot and the winds as his steeds, He went from Olivet to glory—as one goes from deep humiliation to high exaltation.

No. The sin of man has been the grief of God from all eternity—even as the cross of Calvary was a goal in the heart of God from all eternity.

Of Jesus it is affirmed that He was ". . . the Lamb slain from the foundation of the world" (Revelation 13:8)—even as He was loved by the Father ". . . before the foundation of the world . . ." and had "glory which I had with thee before the world was" (John 17:5 and 24), even as God ". . . hath chosen us in him before the foundation of the world, that we should be holy and without blame before him in love:" (Ephesians 1:4).

And there is grief in the heart of Christ today because of man's sin and sinning.

Still, as in all the ages past, all have sinned.

Our hands have sinned—and "all the perfumes of Arabia could not sweeten" our men's strong hands and all our women's lovely little hands.

Our feet have sinned—"all like sheep have gone astray," walking in forbidden paths.

Our ears have sinned—so often are "ears that hear not God's voice"—ears dull of hearing and deaf to calls of distress.

Our eyes have sinned. The "lust of the eyes and the pride of life" are captors—and we captives.

Our hearts have sinned. "The imagination of human hearts is only evil continually." Many are guilty under the shadow of that universal indictment.

Our tongues have sinned—treacherously cutting like blind surgeons—tongues that are worlds of iniquity set on the fires of hell, touching lips with adder's poison under them (Psalms 140:3).

Our shoulders have sinned; they are often withdrawn from daily cross-bearing or from bearing the loads of noble enterprises, even as the nobles of Tekoa ". . . put not their necks to the work of their Lord" (Nehemiah 3:5).

Our knees have sinned; they have pressed the floor of the prayer closet so little—or they have bowed to some worldly Baal.

Our arms have sinned—they have not been placed around the lost sheep, and have not in love embraced the prodigals.

By word, by thought, by deed, by imagination, by commission, by omission, by sleep in harvest time, by secret sin and by open sin, we have crucified the Son of God afresh and have put him to an open shame (Hebrews 6:6).

We are lumps of corruption, masses of unworthiness, and heaps of sin, platters clean only on the outside, with much profession oft, and little possession oft; measuring inches oft, when God demands yards and miles; weighing ounces oft, when God demands and desires pounds and tons; striking six oft, when God wants full twelve always; shining like wee candles struggling against contrary winds when God wants bright shining.

Achan, Pharoah, King Saul, David, Judas, the Prodigal—all said: "I have sinned." So must we! So *do* we say—now. We have denied like Peter. We have betrayed like Judas. We have doubted like Thomas. We have grown stubborn like King Saul. We have given the enemies of the Lord occasion to blaspheme, and have made the way of truth to be evil spoken of. Yes!

"For all have sinned, and come short of the glory of God;" (Romans 3:23). "Wherefore, as by one man sin entered into the world, and death by sin; and so death passed upon all men for that all have sinned:" (Romans 5:12).

"If we say that we have not sinned, we make him a liar, and his word is not in us" (I John 1:10). "All our righteousness is as filthy rags"—if we lay claim to salvation by it. Faithfulness needed, we have been false—too many times. Heroism needed, we have shown cowardice—too many times. Humbleness needed, we have shown pride—too many days, forgetting that God resisteth the proud (James 4:6).

Volunteers called for, we have served only through conscription and pressing coercion—all too often. Applied Christianity is needed—but we have been content with implied Christianity. Devotional vitality demanded and we have been content with mere formality. Yes! The wisdom which is earthly, sensual, devilish, we have often manifested instead of the wisdom which is from above.

No man, with words most skillfully combined and most eloquently spoken, can describe the shameful failure and deep misery and loss that comes to those who are under Satan's yoke and who have the claims of sin upon them. The eagle chained and confined in a chicken coop is not more unhappy than the man carrying the burden and guilt of his sins that haunt him like Banquo's ghost tormented Macbeth. Sin to man's mind is worse than a torture rack to man's body.

That brings me now gratefully to consider:

2. THE GREAT TEST, JUSTIFICATION: Justification shows how God was put to a test. God was not put to a test when He placed the sun in His tabernacle in the heavens and rolled the shining stars off the palm and finger tips of His creative hand and traced the channels for the rolling rivers and scooped out earthen areas in which the tumultuous seas unceasingly play.

> Who hath measured the waters in the hollow of his hand, and meted out heaven with the span, and comprehended the dust of the earth in a measure, and weighed the mountains in scales, and the hills in a balance? (Isaiah 40:12).

But when God was faced with the problem of saving—of justifying—rebellious man, He faced that which was the very test of the Infinite—Infinite omniscience and omnipotence. Why a test? How could He remain just and yet justify the sinner who had violated His just law?

Is not the law of the Lord just?

Is not the administration of that law perfect?

Must not God be careful how He justifies the man who has broken that unswervingly just and perfect law?

Yea, verily!

Has God any reason to *recall* or *explain* or *alter* His law?
No indeed!

Is God under obligation to do anything else but allow His righteous law to move on in its righteousness and so condemn the evil doer? No, sir!

Yet God, the Just, treats as righteous the unjust—even though David said: ". . . in Thy sight shall no man living be justified" (Psalms 143:2).

Sinners can be—and are—justified freely by grace, through faith, wholly apart from works.

But what *is* justification?

Dr. Edgar Young Mullins said: "Justification is a judicial act of God in which he declares the sinner free from condemnation, and restores him to divine favor."

W. T. Conner says: "Justification is the act of God in which the sinner, hitherto condemned on account of his sin, upon conditions of faith in Christ, is forgiven and received into divine favor."

Writes Dr. S. E. Anderson: "Justification is our Bill of Rights to the riches of Christian rejoicing with its rejoicing unspeakable and full of glory." (From Romans 5:11.) (In *The Pilot,* by permission.)

I say that justification is the act or decree of God whereby any sinner anywhere through faith in Christ is cleared of all guilt before God and declared righteous by God and looked upon by God as though that sinner had never sinned, as though he were altogether the righteousness of God. Justification is a transfer of a sinner from the state of sin, damnation, and death, to a state of righteousness, salvation, and eternal life. "For he hath made him to be sin for us, who knew no sin; that we might be made the righteousness of God in him" (II Corinthians 5:21).

Justification is more than forgiveness of sins.

Justification is to have every vestige of guilt removed.

To be justified means that I, as a believer, stand before God "just-as-if-I'd-never-sinned-at-all." Justification concerns our judicial *position*—not our spiritual *condition*.

Says Wendell Loveless: "If the believer will realize that to be justified means to be cleared of all guilt, he will never spend any time in anxiety over past sins—for when God justifies the sinner, he forgets all his sins."

Forgiveness is the removal of the penalty of our sins while justification is the removal of the charge of guilt which once stood against us.

The two-fold aspect of justification is clearance from the guilt of the acts of sin (Acts 13:39) and clearance from the guilt of the nature of sin (Romans 6:7).

If I am arrested under suspicion by others that I committed a crime and am hailed into court, where I declare my innocence, my lawyer calls many witnesses who testify that I was miles away when the offense was committed. My innocence is completely established. By the declaration of the judge, I leave the court without a stain upon my character. In other words, being innocent, I am completely justified.

But if I am guilty of the offense for which I was arrested and brought into court, there are some extenuating circumstances. It is my first offense. I was drawn rather coercively into the offense against my better judgment. The judge rebukes and warns me, then discharges me. Without any penalty being inflicted. I leave the court a free man. Forgiven am I, but not cleared of the charge.

Now that is the difference between justification and forgiveness. But we must remember that, amongst men, only the innocent can be justified and the guilty forgiven.

But the glory of the gospel is that it shows how God can do what is impossible amongst men. He can justify the ungodly, and that when there are no extenuating circumstances. He can take a vile, depraved sinner and not only forgive him but clear him of every charge so completely that the challenge may be rung out and be forever unanswerable. "Who shall lay anything to the charge of God's elect? It is God that justifieth" (Romans 8:33).

Thus we can now say that, according to Bible usage, justification is the act of declaring and counting and pronouncing one righteous—

free from guilt and exposure to punishment—on account of the finished substitutionary work of Jesus.

Legal justification is the act of declaring a person righteous or innocent according to the strict demands of the law—or the act of acquitting a person from the charge of a crime.

"If there be a controversy between men, and they come into judgment, that the judges may judge them; then they shall justify the righteous, and condemn the wicked" (Deuteronomy 25:1).

But we are considering now:

3. THE GREAT NEED—GOSPEL JUSTIFICATION: Gospel justification is that act or decree of God made in heaven whereby He declares a sinner righteous through the merits of a substitute.

(A) *It includes Pardon.* And pardon is release from a penalty.

(B) *It includes Forgiveness.* And forgiveness means the giving up of an inward feeling of injury or resentment—the removing of a feeling of anger and the restoring of a feeling of favor and affection. "Be it known unto you therefore, men and brethren, that through this man is preached unto you the forgiveness of sins: And by him all that believe are justified from all things, from which he could not be justified by the law of Moses" (Acts 13:38-39).

(C) *It includes Remission.* And remission is the *judicial* putting away of sin. "To him give all the prophets witness, that through his name whosoever believeth in him shall receive remission of sins" (Acts 10:43). Doubtless it also includes "forgetting"—or putting away from the mind, remembering no more!

(D) *It includes Propitiation.* And propitiation is the act of appeasing the wrath and winning the favor of an offended person. "Whom God hath set forth to be a propitiation through faith in his blood, to declare his righteousness for the remission of sins that are past, through the forbearance of God;" (Romans 3:25).

(E) *It includes Reconciliation.* "And, having made peace through the blood of his cross, by him to reconcile all things unto himself; by him, I say, whether they be things in earth, or things in heaven. And you, that were sometime alienated and enemies in your mind by wicked works, yet now hath he reconciled In the body of his flesh through death, to present you holy and unblameable and unreprove-able in his sight:" (Colossians 1:20–22).

There is a slight difference between each of these, although they are different phases of one great act, and, as far as God is concerned, they take place at the same time. Humanly speaking, one may receive pardon without forgiveness. He may also receive pardon and forgiveness without remission. Remission, propitiation and reconciliation, besides being definite acts of God based upon the finished work of Jesus, also represent phases of the work of Jesus which made these acts possible. As Judge, God pardons; as Father, He forgives.

To be justified is to be made righteous.

To be made righteous is a great need.

When a man is justified, it is declared of him that he has never committed an offense. For stealing, a man is put in prison. He serves his sentence. He is then freed. He has paid the penalty, but he is still guilty. His prison term stands against his record. Though free, after serving his sentence, he has not been *justified*.

A man kills a man. He is given a life sentence of imprisonment at hard labor. In twenty years, he is pardoned. He is now free. He has been pardoned, but he has not been justified. It is still known of him that he is guilty of killing a man. But every real Christian has been justified—*counted as completely righteous before God*.

There is a great need for justification on the part of man— when all the world is guilty before God—because even those who seem to have been more righteous than most and holy above many others have ever been those who have acknowledged great transgressions.

Job, looked upon by many as perfect and weighing much on God's scales of righteous evaluations, said: "Wherefore I abhor myself, and repent in dust and ashes" (Job 42:6). "If I wash myself with snow water, and make my hands never so clean; Yet shall thou plunge me in the ditch, and mine own clothes shall abhor me" (Job 9:30–31).

David, the sweetest singer of Israel, said: "Purge me with hyssop, and I shall be clean: wash me, and I shall be whiter than snow" (Psalms 51:7).

John the Baptist, lion-hearted and eagle-eyed, who descended upon the iniquities of his day with a torch in one hand and a sword in the other—to whom was given the delicate task of interpreting the voice of betrothal as the friend of the bridegroom—said to Jesus: ". . . I have need to be baptized of thee, . . ." (Matthew 3:14). And there is Peter, the Pentecostal preacher, who said: ". . . Depart from me; for I am a sinful man, O Lord" (Luke 5:8).

There is Isaiah, in whose preaching were the thunders of Sinai and the foregleams of Calvary, who said ". . . I am a man of unclean lips, . . ." (Isaiah 6:5). This shows that man has need of being justified by God—of being looked upon as righteous by the Lord.

Men need justification. And after justification, our need of forgiveness is then associated with our filial position—and we are then forgiven as children, not as unconverted sinners. "If we confess our sins, he is faithful and just to forgive us our sins, and to cleanse us from all unrighteousness" (I John 1:9).

This could not be said of the unconverted—because it is by God's mercy, not his faithfulness, that the sinner is forgiven. And so while forgiveness cancels the penalty of sin, justification provides a permanent standing before God. And that standing is ours before God through our Lord Jesus Christ. *No charge whatever is placed against us.*

4. THE GREAT PREDICATION—ACCEPTANCE OF CHRIST BY FAITH: Glorious truth we have here. "For he hath made him to be sin for us, who knew no sin; that we might be made the righteousness of God in him" (II Corinthians 5:21). Meaning what? Meaning that on the cross, Jesus, the perfectly righteous One, was judged as unrighteous that we, the unrighteous, might be judged as righteous through faith in the Lord Jesus Christ. This righteousness of God—this justification—we can not provide for ourselves. We can not by our own goodness. "How can a man then be justified with God?" Our justification is predicated upon our acceptance of Christ by faith as the One

who took our place on the cross—Christ who is Heaven's grace for earth's guilt.

For four thousand years, God had been searching for a good man and finally wound up by saying "There is none righteous—no not one." Men babble of their goodness—like a parrot chattering noisily, without intelligence. Men spread out their robes of self-righteousness —like some peacock proudly preening pretty plumage. Men display their goodness—like a drum major cavorting in a parade. "How then can a man be justified with God?"

Not by *character*. A man who says he will be justified with God by developing a fine character makes a counterfeit out of character by passing it for more than it is worth. "How then can a man be justified with God?"

Not by *good works*. "Knowing that a man is not justified by the works of the law, but by the faith of Jesus Christ, even we have believed in Jesus Christ, that we might be justified by the faith of Christ, and not by the works of the law: for by the works of the law shall no flesh be justified" (Galatians 2:16). "For by grace are ye saved through faith; and that not of yourselves: it is the gift of God: Not of works, lest any man should boast" (Ephesians 2:8–9).

In the *law* a righteousness *from* man is required. In *Christ,* a righteousness *for* man is revealed.

We are not righteous in ourselves.

God provides salvation through the righteousness of another— and this righteousness is received by faith in that Other. We are not righteous in ourselves. We cannot acquire righteousness on the principle of keeping the law. There is no power to save either in ourselves or through law. We are like a man on a train who has lost his ticket and his pocketbook as well, so that he can not buy another ticket. We are both destitute of a righteousness that will save—and helpless to attain it.

The righteousness of God we have in Christ is that righteousness which His own righteousness required Him to require—the sum total of all that God commands, demands, approves, and provides.

That righteousness is the righteousness which the Father requires, the Son provides, the Holy Spirit convinces of, and faith secures. "That, according as it is written, he that glorieth, let him glory in the Lord" (I Corinthians 1:31).

But how can justification come from God? Will God say that His law was unjust—and that because of its imperfections, He pardons violation of His law? Will God say He blundered when He attached a fixed and just penalty to offenses? Then has God become fickle and imperfect—and we have lost the infinite Jehovah. Can God play fast and loose with men's sins? Then has God ceased to be the holy Arbiter of the destinies of men.

Bishop John Newton once said: "If a man violate the perfect law of God, there is for him no pardon, but suffering must be endured by him, or an adequate substitute."

But where in all the world can you find an adequate substitute? For it is not the payment of a fine with gold that will suffice. It is not the bearing of a term in prison where heroism may sustain one. It is sin we face. It is a world's sin we confront. And it is the atoning for a whole world guilty before God that constitutes the problem.

That brings us to consider:

5. THE GREAT HOW—HOW MAN IS JUSTIFIED WITH GOD: How is man to get this justification which is so necessary? In justification we have a complete atonement available. "And not only so, but we also joy in God through our Lord Jesus Christ, by whom we have now received the atonement" (Romans 5:11).

In justification our death penalty has been revoked. That death penalty was transferred from us to the body of Christ, our Saviour.

The sins of Adam were imputed to us.

Wherefore, as by one man sin entered into the world, and death by sin; and so death passed upon all men, for that all have sinned: (Romans 5:12).

Then on Calvary our sins were imputed to Christ.

For when we were yet without strength, in due time Christ died for the ungodly (Romans 5:6).

All we like sheep have gone astray; we have turned every one to his own way; and the Lord hath laid on him the iniquity of us all (Isaiah 53:6).

Then the righteousness of Christ has been imputed to us.

Therefore as by the offence of one judgment came upon all men to condemnation; even so by the righteousness of one the free gift came upon all men unto justification of life (Romans 5:18).

In justification, we have immunity from future condemnation.

There is therefore now no condemnation to them which are in Christ Jesus, who walk not after the flesh, but after the Spirit (Romans 8:1). Who shall lay anything to the charge of God's elect? It is God that justifieth. Who is he that condemeth? It is Christ that died, yea rather, that is risen again, who is even at the right hand of God, who also maketh intercession for us (Romans 8:33-34).

In justification, we have adoption. Our adoption as children into God's family was made possible—legalized, ratified, sealed—because we were declared righteous in God's sight.

For ye have not received the spirit of bondage again to fear; but ye have received the Spirit of adoption, whereby we cry, Abba, Father (Romans 8:15).

If we had once been judicially included in that diabolical family, concerning which Jesus once said: "Ye are of your father the devil," we are forever and irrevocably transferred into God's family by our justification.

In justification, our sonship is established, sealed, and secured.

The Spirit beareth witness with our spirit, that we are the children of God (Romans 8:16).

And grieve not the holy Spirit of God, whereby ye are sealed unto the day of redemption (Ephesians 4:30).

For I am persuaded, that neither death, nor life, nor angels, nor principalities, nor powers, nor things present, nor things to come, Nor height, nor depth, nor any other creature, shall be able to separate us from the love of God, which is in Christ Jesus our Lord (Romans 8: 38–39).

The illustration of Captain Dreyfus is apropos in this connection. You will remember how he was condemned in front of his own regiment, how his sword was taken from him, the epaulettes were torn from his shoulders, his uniform stripped from him, and then he was imprisoned. Afterwards, by the influence of some friends, a trial was brought about, and ultimately he was pardoned and set free. You might ask: What more could he want? How wonderful that he was forgiven and liberated! But Captain Dreyfus was not satisfied, nor would you have been. He had been publicly degraded.

Another trial was held, and this time he was reinstated,—more than that, he was given the position in his regiment that he would have occupied had he never been condemned. It was reckoned that had he never left his regiment he would have risen to the rank of Colonel, and, therefore, he was made Colonel. *This is justification*. And God in His wonderful mercy puts us into that position, just as though we had never sinned. "For he hath made him to be sin for us, who knew no sin; that we might be made the righteousness of God in him" (II Corinthians 5:21).

The great marvel of the Gospel, the great triumph of redemption, is that God can declare to be righteous those who are personally not righteous—that He can justify the sinner, not as deeming him a law *keeper*, but even while He judges him a law *breaker*.

But *how* does this marvelous justification come?

How does it become a personal possession?

How are men justified?

Men are justified by the grace of God. "Being justified freely by his grace through the redemption that is in Christ Jesus:" (Romans 3:24).

Men are justified by the blood of Jesus. ". . . being now justified by his blood, we shall be saved from wrath through him" (Romans 5:9).

Men are justified by the righteousness of Jesus. "... by the righteousness of one the free gift came upon all men unto justification of life" (Romans 5:18).

Men are justified by the obedience of Jesus. "... by the obedience of one shall many be made righteous" (Romans 5:19). His obedience was unto death, even the death of the cross (Philippians 2:8).

Men are justified by the name of Jesus. "... ye are justified in the name of the Lord Jesus ..." (I Corinthians 6:11).

Men are not justified by doing the works of the Law, but by faith in Christ. "Knowing that a man is not justified by the works of the law, but by the faith of Jesus Christ, even we have believed in Jesus Christ, that we might be justified by the faith of Christ, and not by the works of the law: for by the works of the law shall no flesh be justified" (Galatians 2:16).

"... the righteousness of God which is by faith of Jesus Christ unto all and upon all them that believe: ..." (Romans 3:22).

Sinners are justified causatively by God's *grace*—"Being justified freely by his grace through the redemption that is in Christ Jesus:" (Romans 3:24).

Sinners are justified meritoriously by Christ's *blood*—"Much more then, being now justified by his blood, we shall be saved from wrath through him" (Romans 5:9).

Sinners are justified instrumentally by man's faith. "Therefore being justified by faith, we have peace with God through our Lord Jesus Christ:" (Romans 5:1).

"Be it known unto you therefore, men and brethren, that through this man is preached unto you the forgiveness of sins: And by him all that believe are justified from all things, from which ye could not be justified by the law of Moses" (Acts 13:38-39).

That brings us now to think of:

6. THE GREAT PROPITIATION—CHRIST:

Being justified freely by his grace through the redemption that is in Christ Jesus: Whom God hath set forth to be a propitiation through faith in his blood, to declare his righteousness for the remission of sins that are past, through the forbearance of God; To declare, I say, at this time his righteousness: that he might be just, and the justifier of him which believeth in Jesus (Romans 3:24-26).

And he is the propitiation for our sins: and not for ours only, but also for the sins of the whole world (I John 2:2).

Herein is love, not that we loved God, but that he loved us, and sent his Son to be the propitiation for our sins (I John 4:10).

God has required a sinless sacrifice to satisfy His righteousness and holiness. Obedience to the law will not suffice. "Therefore by the deeds of the law there shall no flesh be justified in his sight: for by the law is the knowledge of sin" (Romans 3:20).

When sin is understood, the sinner knows that he is totally void of anything that will make him right in the sight of God.

Who then is sufficient?

All the waters of the Nile and the Rhine and the Mississippi with the Jordan added are useless here.

An angel's arm is too short, for God chargeth the very angels with folly. All the perfumes of Arabia can not sweeten the sinner's hand.

Could the sinner's tears forever flow, could the sinner's zeal no languor know, all for sin cannot atone. *Christ must save—and Christ alone.*

The penalty of sin must be borne by the sinner or by an adequate substitute. The only adequate substitute is Jesus—Jesus who was, as we know, *prefigured* by the ever-flowing streams of red and sacrificial blood, who was *foreshadowed* by millions of offerings on countless altars slain, who "loved by the Father before the foundation of the world," was foretold by the prophets since the world began.

Upon this Jesus, who came down from the heights of deity to the depths of humanity, John the Baptist looked and saw how all the altars of Judaism and all the prophecies culminated and met and ended in the Lamb of God who taketh away the sin of the world. For Christ bore our sins in His own body on the tree. Christ, who on the cross became for us all whom God must judge, was the infinite sacrifice offered—a sacrifice which enabled God to remit the penalty of guilt to all believers.

Jesus, by the sacrifice of Himself, could redeem as many fallen worlds as God has stars in His heaven—because the infinite merit of the Son of God atones for the sins of the whole world.

Once Plato and Socrates talked under the sunny skies of old Greece about the great problem of sin. Plato said to Socrates: "God may forgive a deliberate sin, but I do not know how He can do it." Yet the Apostle John, knowing what Plato had failed to discover, said: ". . . the blood of Jesus Christ his Son cleanseth us from all sin" (I John 1:7).

Somebody tells how Rowland Hill, the last time he preached, remained in the church at the close of the service until all had gone but the caretaker, who stood watching the preacher as he walked up and down the aisle of the empty church and slowly repeated to himself:

> This I shall find,
> For such is his mind —
> He wont be in glory
> And leave me behind.

Why did Rowland Hill know that? Because he had learned another verse of that same hymn:

> He bore on the tree
> The burden for me;
> And both sinner
> And Surety are free.

Rowland Hill saw the propitiation atonement of Jesus opening a door wide enough to let a guilty world go out into the sunshine of satisfied justice—and into the light of the reconciled countenance of God.

I remember how Billy Sunday told of the governor of a state who went into the penitentiary—and he especially wanted to see a certain man. He saw him, and he sat in the man's cell. And he talked with the prisoner, but he concealed his identity until the interview had ended—and he was gone. Then one of the guards said: "Do you know that the governor of the state was just talking to you?"

"Oh, my God!" said the man. "Had I known that, how on bended knee, I would have pleaded with him for pardon. I would not have let him go until he had pardoned me."

The Saviour of sinners comes into our churches.

The Saviour is in this church this very hour.

And He can not conceal His identity—because He has scars in His palms, and His brow bears the trace of thorns—and He offers sinners a pardon written in His own blood and says: "Take it from me. Accept it. Be more than pardoned, more than forgiven. Be justified—*now*."

IV

Forgetting Things Behind

Brethren, I count not myself to have apprehended: but this one thing I do, forgetting those things which are behind, and reaching forth unto those things which are before. I press toward the mark. . . . (Philippians 3:13-14).

We are to think a bit of:

1. The Sin of Forgetting:

In no realm is the sin of forgetting—of having a weak remembrance as to God's goodness and mercies—so strong and so relentless as in the spiritual realm. In no realm is the tendency to thoughtlessness so relentless and strong as in the spiritual realm. Thus the Bible —from beginning to end, in history, in law, in prayers, in parables, in prophecy, in proverb, line upon line, precept upon precept, here a little and there a little—strives to put us in remembrance of our duty to God and to man.

In that bold and brilliant parable of Lazarus and the rich man there flashed out like vivid lightning the awful words of Abraham to one whose sin had been a sin of forgetting.

But Abraham said, Son, remember that thou in thy lifetime receivedst thy good things, and likewise Lazarus evil things: but now he is comforted, and thou art tormented (Luke 16:25).

In a solemn passage, Jesus uses an allusion dark with tragedy: "Remember Lot's wife" (Luke 17:32). Jude says: "But, beloved, remember ye the words which were spoken before of the apostles of our Lord Jesus Christ;" (Jude 17). The writer of the epistle to the Hebrews says:

Remember them that are in bonds, as bound with them; and them which suffer adversity, as being yourselves also in the body.

Remember them which have the rule over you, who have spoken unto you the word of God: whose faith follow, considering the end of their conversation (Hebrews 13:3, 7).

Writing from prison and chained to a soldier, Paul wrote to the Colossians: ". . . Remember my bonds . . ." (Colossians 4:18) and to the Thessalonians, he wrote: "For ye remember, brethren, our labor and travail: for labouring night and day, because we would not be chargeable unto any of you, we preached unto you the gospel of God" (I Thessalonians 2:9).

To Timothy, Paul writes: "Remember that Jesus Christ of the seed of David was raised from the dead according to my gospel:" (II Timothy 2:8). And Peter writes, lest the sin of thoughtlessness be the undoing of some: "Yea, I think it meet, as long as I am in this tabernacle, to stir you up by putting you in remembrance;" (II Peter 1:13).

God, through Jeremiah, makes this lament:

Can a maid forget her ornaments, or a bride her attire? Yet my people have forgotten me days without number (Jeremiah 2:32).

A voice was heard upon the high places, weeping and supplications of the children of Israel: for they have perverted their way, and they have forgotten the LORD their God (Jeremiah 3:21).

And we read this sad statement: "Of the Rock that begat thee thou art unmindful, and hast forgotten God that formed thee" (Deuteronomy 32:18).

Through Ezekiel, God, as one sobbing, said:

In thee have they taken gifts to shed blood; thou hast taken usury and increase, and thou hast greedily gained of thy neighbours by extortion, and hast forgotten me, saith the Lord GOD (Ezekiel 22:12).

God uttered this rebuke by the inspired writer: "And ye have forgotten the exhortation which speaketh unto you as unto children, My son, despise not thou the chastening of the Lord, nor faint when thou art rebuked of him:" (Hebrews 12:5).

God warns against forgetfulness—and shows that there is such a thing as sinful forgetfulness. Read these words:

Only take heed to thyself, and keep thy soul diligently, lest thou forget the things which thine eyes have seen, and lest they depart from thy heart all the days of thy life: but teach them thy sons, and thy sons' sons; (Deuteronomy 4:9).

Take heed unto yourselves, lest ye forget the covenant of the LORD your God, which he made with you, and make you a graven image, or the likeness of any thing, which the LORD thy God hath forbidden thee (Deuteronomy 4:23).

Then beware lest thou forget the LORD, which brought thee forth out of the land of Egypt, from the house of bondage (Deuteronomy 6:12).

Beware that thou forget not the LORD thy God, in not keeping his commandments, and his judgments, and his statutes, which I command thee this day: (Deuteronomy 8:11).

Then thine heart be lifted up, and thou forget the LORD thy God, which brought thee forth out of the land of Egypt, from the house of bondage; (Deuteronomy 8:14).

And it shall be, if thou do at all forget the LORD thy God, and walk after other gods, and serve them, and worship them, I testify against you this day that ye shall surely perish (Deuteronomy 8:19).

Remember, and forget not, how thou provokedst the LORD thy God to wrath in the wilderness: from the day that thou didst depart out of the land of Egypt, until ye came unto this place, ye have been rebellious against the LORD (Deuteronomy 9:7).

Therefore it shall be, when the LORD thy God hath given thee rest from all thine enemies round about in the land which the LORD thy God giveth thee for an inheritance to possess it, that thou shalt blot out the remembrance of Amalek from under heaven; thou shalt not forget it (Deuteronomy 25:19).

And the covenant that I have made with you ye shall not forget; neither shall ye fear other gods (II Kings 17:38).

For wisdom is better than rubies; and all the things that may be desired are not to be compared to it. I wisdom dwell with prudence, and find out knowledge of witty inventions. The fear of the LORD is to hate evil: pride, and arrogancy, and the evil way, and the froward mouth, do I hate (Proverbs 8:11–13).

The wicked shall be turned into hell, and all the nations that forget God (Psalms 9:17).

Now consider this, ye that forget God, lest I tear you in pieces, and there be none to deliver (Psalms 50:22).

David set forth the shame of forgetting when he wrote:

If I forget thee, O Jerusalem, let my right hand forget her cunning. If I do not remember thee, let my tongue cleave to the roof of my mouth; if I prefer not Jerusalem above my chief joy (Psalms 137:5–6).

Solomon taught: "Get wisdom, get understanding: forget it not; neither decline from the words of my mouth" (Proverbs 4:5).

God, through Jeremiah, said:

How long shall this be in the heart of the prophets that prophesy lies? yea, they are prophets of the deceit of their own heart; Which think to cause my people to forget my name by their dreams which they tell every man to his neighbour, as their fathers have forgotten my name for Baal (Jeremiah 23:26–27).

God warns men in these words:

My people are destroyed for lack of knowledge: because thou hast rejected knowledge, I will also reject thee, that thou shalt be no priest to me: seeing thou hast forgotten the law of thy God, I will also forget thy children (Hosea 4:6).

The LORD hath sworn by the excellency of Jacob, Surely I will never forget any of their works (Amos 8:7).

But we have these comforting words:

Can a woman forget her suckling child, that she should not have compassion on the son of her womb? yea, they may forget, yet will not I forget thee (Isaiah 49:15).

For God is not unrighteous to forget your work and labour of love, which ye have shewed toward his name, in that ye have ministered to the saints, and do minister (Hebrews 6:10).

When he maketh inquisition for blood, he remembereth them: he forgetteth not the cry of the humble (Psalms 9:12).

Yes, though tragic is the truth, men forget Jesus Christ. We remember sport and many—who know how many home runs Babe Ruth knocked, and how many rounds Dempsey fought, and how many tennis matches Schmiszu won, and how the race came out between Cornell or Yale, and what Dan Patch's pacing record is, and what the world's mile record is, and how many wrestling matches "Strangler" Lewis won—do not know how many books are in the Bible, or how many problems are before the preacher, or how many hours Christ was on the cross!

Many remember the thrilling discovery of America by Columbus, but forget the wonderful narrative of Jesus' rediscovery, or the revelation of God, saying: "The Father and I are one."

Many remember Alexander who wept for more worlds to conquer, but forget Jesus who wept because Jerusalem refused to receive Him as Son of God and Saviour of men.

Many remember Washington at Valley Forge praying in the snow, but forget Jesus praying in Gethsemane when the roots of His divine emotion put forth their crimson tears.

Many remember "Mad" Anthony Wayne storming the heights of Stony Point, but forget Jesus with His calm face set like a flint toward the cross of Calvary, where, assaulted by all the hatreds of men and all the furies of hell, He "bore our sins in his own body on the tree."

Many, reading biography and autobiography, learn much and remember many things of men. But they are prone to forget Christ's public ministry of three years, His matchless teaching, His habits of constant communion with the Father, His love for little children, His affection for and sympathy with the outcast, His complete freedom from artificial standards, His understanding of and kindness to the common people, the stroke after stroke which fell so tragically the last few days of His earthly career, His makeshift trial before the tribunals of men, the cruel blows in His face, the malicious mocking and murder of the cross.

Consider, in the light of what we have just said:

2. THE WISDOM AND RIGHTEOUSNESS OF FORGETFULNESS: Seeing then that there is the sin of forgetfulness against which God warns and which He condemns and punishes—is it strange that we come now to consider the wisdom and the righteousness of forgetfulness— of forgetting the things that are behind? Perhaps strange is this urging from the Apostle Paul when we have learned much of the power of remembrance—of the power of recall.

Though the power of recall in many is full of wonder and interest for us, there is a difference in man's power to recall. Themistocles could call the name of twenty thousand citizens of Athens. Ben Jonson said he could repeat all he had ever written, and whole books he had reviewed. In 1851, a Corsican youth repeated thirty-six thousand words after once hearing them. Macaulay could repeat the whole of "Paradise Lost." Senator Tillman of South Carolina could recite page after page of Shakespeare. Humboldt never forgot anything. Of Webster's "Answer to Hayne," it was said, "Every thing he had seen or heard, read or thought, stood before him in perfect order."

A cause for marvel is that men have such power of recall. But that power of recall—of remembrance—is often as a lash, as a whip upon a naked back. Each terrified thought of life is not simply a review of the past, but a frightful cavalcade thundering through the soul—and the past stands before us a very present thing.

Think of the rich man about whom Jesus spoke. The power of recall—of remembrance—was a lash to him. Abraham said: "Son, remember!" That was the word which kindled such a fire in his soul as rivers of water could not quench. It set every nerve a-thrill with anguish. It is memory, the power of recall, that drives men to yield to the officers of the law, and to take their own lives.

Cain slew his brother staining the earth with his blood. But it was the power of recall, of remembrance, the remembrance of what he had done which made him—when he found that God's decree was that he should be a fugitive and vagabond upon the face of the earth (Genesis 4:12)—to cry out ". . . My punishment is greater than I can bear" (Genesis 4:13).

Memory, the power of recall, made Macbeth see Banquo's ghost at the table and made Lady Macbeth wail that all the perfumes of Arabia could not sweeten her little hand.

But Paul urges us to exercise the power, to show the wisdom of being forgetful of the things that are behind and past.

The most remarkable Christian of all the centuries was—and is —Saul of Tarsus, the Apostle Paul. He was and is the greatest single credential that Christ's gospel has ever produced. An executioner of Christians, he met Jesus on the road to Damascus and was converted —regenerated. And thus, through the change in the path of his destiny, he made a voyage from the tea-cup of himself into the ocean of God's self. A slave of the temporal, he became a king of the eternal. In the blaze that smote him to his knees, he saw "the light . . . of the glory of God in the face of Jesus Christ" (II Corinthians 4:6). For him the first flame of the trail of glory which he was destined to leave across the Gentile world was kindled quickly. Till that hour, he had been a mournful monotony of jangling inharmonies, missing life's central melody—because he was the victim of dawdling ditties. But that day, so momentously significant, he came out from

> The vain pomp and shows,
> From the pride that overflows
> And the false conceits of men,
> From all the narrow rules
> And subtleties of schools
> And the craft of tongue and pen
> Into the life of Christ and the life in Christ.
>   (Author unknown.)

What an hour, when Saul was new-born! Then a Christian ambition became supreme; and in the fierceness of his desire he drew every minor yearning to the central purpose like tributaries converging upon the main stream. From the time when it was "sunset in Damascus but dawn in the life of Saul," he counted all things but loss that he might know Jesus and the power of his resurrection and the fellowship of his suffering (Philippians 3:7–10).

The revelation of the Lord led to the revelation of the limitless landscape. Greatly he believed, greatly he was saved, greatly he lived. For weal or woe, come prison or scourge, stoning or exile or the cross itself, he, Saul, was Christ's man. And for Christ he was in peril of his life in Damascus, coldly suspected by his fellow believers in Jerusalem, persecuted in Antioch, stoned in Lystra, assaulted in Iconium, beaten with many stripes in Philippi, attacked by a lewd and envious crowd in Thessalonica, pursued by callous enmity at Berea, despised in Athens, blasphemed in Corinth, exposed to the fierce wrath of the Ephesians, bound with chains in Jerusalem, and sent as a prisoner to Rome.

Now, in Philippians 3:13, he gives one of the secrets of his marvellous life and ministry. That verse reveals the explanatory dynamic of his career.

". . . forgetting those things which are behind." That is a hard thing to do because memory makes it hard to forget the past. Memory is the faculty of bringing back into consciousness that which has passed out of it. Memory peoples the present with the people of the past. Memory walks in the silent city of bygones. Memory stands amid the graves where lie buried experiences and achievements of other years. Memory speaks in the shadowy world of departed spirits —and as it speaks the dead are suffused with life again. Memory is the angel of the resurrection on this side of the grave.

Once, long ago, Jesus stood at the tomb of Lazarus and said to the man that had lain dead for days: "Come Forth"—and Lazarus came up from the grave again to live and speak in the present. Memory achieves a miracle just like this, as it stands at the mouth of some tomb wherein have slept, not for four days but perhaps for four decades, the pulseless forms of life's vanished experiences. With the sovereign command of God, memory says "Come Forth"—and the dead live again. Old faces, old voices, old friendships steal forth out of the shadows and stand with us in the light of the present.

Aristotle said: "Memory is the scribe of the soul."

Thomas B. Hood wrote: "Memory is a golden thread linking in one all the achievements of the mind and all the experiences of the heart."

James I. Vance wrote: "Treat memory kindly, it becomes a guardian angel. Treat it ill, it becomes a demon spirit, mocking you with fiendish glee."

Bishop Basil said: "Memory is the cabinet of imagination, the treasury of reason, the registry of conscience, the council chamber of thought."

A great scholar said: "Memory is life's battle abbey on whose walls are hung the flags that tell the struggles through which we have marched."

Newell Dwight Hillis taught: "Memory is the heart's mausoleum in which are treasured the loves that made golden the days that have dropped into the sunset."

While it is a duty to forget the things behind, the difficulty of so doing is ever with us. And it is great—almost as great as erasing carving from marble or engraving from bronze. 'Tis hard to forget the things that are behind—to have a mental graveyard for them. Paul's yesterday held the memory of intolerance, hatred, cruelty, slaughterous thoughts, crime, even murder. The past brought distress and torment. Instead of being a place of refuge, a tower into which he could retreat from present disasters, it became a wound that would not heal, a tomb full of ghastly recollections, a closet full of skeletons.

Many a man has had Paul's experience in that memory is a clog and a torment and a hindrance—reproachful whispers on the wind. Here is a man who betrayed honor in his youth. Here is a man who refused knowledge. Here is a woman who refused counsel and made a foolish marriage. Here are men who have sinned against the body —men who threw away in Folly's Court and Carnal Pleasure's Mart the wealth God gave them at the start. Here are men betrayed into errors of judgment. Here are men who cheated. Here are men who have eaten with a crook and slept with a crook and companioned every second of every minute with a crook, because they were themselves crooks.

At the threshold of this year—with many things gone forever

into the Tomb of Time and with many things not yet come to us from the Womb of Time—God would have us to show:

3. FORGETFULNESS OF OUR BLUNDERS: Yes, our blunders—no matter how aggravated, no matter how evil, no matter how many, no matter how grievous. Brooding on yesterday's blunders tends toward morbidness—and dishonors God. Dragging the dead out of the grave destroys health—and is a sin against one's own soul. Dragging skeletons out of the closet is a hideous business—and foolish. "Let the dead stay buried." Forget the things that are behind.

Else you will show that you are as unkind to yourself and as foolish as Charles II who, with pomp and pageantry, ordered Oliver Cromwell's bones exhumed and the skeleton hanged between two thieves at Tyburn to satisfy his hatred. For twelve years Cromwell's skull was elevated upon a pole above Westminster Hall, where it stood exposed to the rain of twelve summers and the snows of twelve winters.

In the Bible, the emphasis has been placed repeatedly upon the one great word "Remember." All the way from Moses to the latest of the apostles, men are saying "Do not forget." That is only half the message. Side by side with the exhortation to remember is the injunction to forget.

Isaiah, the preacher in whose prophecy and preaching were thunders of Sinai and foregleams of Calvary, speaks almost the same words as the Apostle Paul when he says: "Remember ye not the former things, neither consider the things of old" (Isaiah 43:18). This means we are to dismiss from our minds many things which are behind.

Ezekiel, with burning passion, pleads with his countrymen to remember Egypt no more: "They shall also strip thee out of thy clothes, and take away thy fair jewels. Thus will I make thy lewdness to cease from thee, and thy whoredom brought from the land of Egypt: so that thou shalt not lift up thine eyes unto them, nor remember Egypt any more" (Ezekiel 23:26–27).

There are some things to be remembered. There are some things to be forgotten. No man who wishes to achieve success can afford to do useless and weakening things. One of the most useless of all habits is that of dragging along too much of one's past, like one chained to a dead body. It handicaps a man in the race. It takes from him his strength. Many a man has been fatally crippled and paralyzed simply by carrying along some things he ought to have let go.

Blunders! We have all committed them. We made them when we were little children. We made them when young men and young women. We made them when adults, which is somewhat more surprising. Some will say: "If I had taken the left road instead of right." "If I had put my money here and not put it there." "If I had obtained an education or a different kind of education." If I had done something else! Let us forget our mistakes and remember them no more forever. Let us stand on top of them and reach out for higher things. How often people say: "What a fool *I* was!" "What a FOOL I was!" "What a fool I WAS!" The next time you catch yourself saying that, change the tense of your verb. Do not say, "What a fool I *was!*" But say this: "What a fool I *am* to keep everlastingly saying 'What a fool I was.'" A man never displays his folly more conspicuously than when he is using up his strength and time in crying over spilt milk.

Certainly we are right and wise to:

4. FORGET OUR LOSSES: It takes a man a long time to learn how to walk a tight rope, or play a position on a team, or solve a puzzle, or carry a load up a hill. And it may take a struggle to forget your losses. We must learn to get past them. It is a painful and tragic sight to see a strong, alert man singing his dirges and chanting his Jeremiads because he lost some property or money, none of which he can take with him when he dies. No man is to whine and mope and go down because there are losses here and there.

This does not mean we are to forget and never recall those whom we have loved and lost awhile. Must we go no more into the secret chambers of memory and think of our beloved and saved dead? Must we try to erase their images from the tablets of our hearts? Our redeemed dead are not behind us, but before us. And though it may seem a long time since we left them back yonder, the passing years are not carrying us farther from them, but closer.

Some lose money through their own carelessness. Some lose money through rascality of others. Don't sit down and moan! It will not regain a lost dollar. Don't lie down and lose sleep! It will not regain a dime. Do not grieve yourself to the grave! It is sad to lose money, sadder it is to lose good sense. What is the sense in grieving over a thing that is gone irretrievably?

If a man could get his hand on money by simply reaching into the past, that would be a sensible thing to do. But when a man can grasp nothing but a shadow, a shadow with poison in it, which will stunt and blast his soul—how foolish for him to keep grasping at the shadow!

Then, too, if we are going to be really Christian and show the Christlike spirit, we must:

5. FORGET OUR INJURIES: We cannot go through life without being wounded, for life is a battle ground. Sooner or later somebody hurts us. Some hurt us unintentionally. Some hurt us maliciously and on purpose. Somebody lies about us—because he is a liar. Somebody tries to tell the truth about us, but does not succeed—because the good we do is oft unappreciated. Somebody misrepresents us—because he does not understand us. Somebody insults us—because he does not like Christ. Somebody slights us—because of selfishness. Somebody works against us, or tries to undermine us, or endeavours to tarnish our name, or to weaken our influence. We are opposed by those who do not hesitate to do things which are tricky and mean. What shall we do with all these slights, these insults, these offenses? Forget them! Brooding on them uses strength needlessly. A single evil resentment weighs more than a ton of lead. It is a millstone around a man's neck and will drown him in the depths of the sea. For hate is the heaviest thing in God's universe—because it is most unlike the disposition of God. You cannot carry any of it along with you without depleting your strength. How foolish to carry even a little of it from one year to another. Why not throw it behind your back? Why

not wash the slate clean? You have a great score of offenses, wash the whole score out and begin all over again.

A man is not master of himself, is not free to do his best work, until he can stand on his feet and say: "There is not a soul on earth against whom I could lift my finger with a desire to hurt him, nor is there a single human being whom I have either the time or disposition to hate." Of course, somebody has injured you. Your misfortune would be honeycomb to somebody. But a sense of injury is aggravated by remembrance and a grudge is the heaviest load you ever carried.

Knowing this, shall I keep up an interest in injuries? Knowing this, shall I feed a fever? Knowing this, shall I keep open a sore? Knowing these things, shall I help leprosy to grow?

This was said about Lincoln: "His heart was as big as the world, but in it he had no room for the memory of a wrong."

And why should you make chambers for every skeleton, and, by retrospection, brood upon each blunder, and weep over each mistake and sin? All this injures aspiration as a frost blights young corn. This morbidness cuts the very nerve of character. No wise man saves his old shoes, or puts away his old garments, or treasures the paring of the nails, or sweeps up his hair when the barber has finished shingling it. A wise housewife clears the attic and the garret once a year, lest the cast-off articles become food for moths and a center for disease and contagion. The city has scavengers to cleanse its streets and fling away all remnants of food and daily life. Every man should cleanse his memory from time to time, as the farmer cleanses the spring and fountain, flinging away the leaves and mud that have slowly collected in the water that sustains the daily life. For God's throne is mercy, sympathy and love, and He is faithful and just to forgive man's sins, to rid each Saul of his fetter, and to lend each Paul strength for the morrow's task.

Forbearing one another, and forgiving one another, if any man have a quarrel against any: even as Christ forgave you, so also do ye (Colossians 3:13).

Before Louis XII became King of France he suffered great indignities at the hand of his cousin, Charles VIII. He was slandered, thrown into prison, kept in chains and in constant fear of death.

When he succeeded Charles to the throne, however, his close friends and advisers urged him to seek revenge for all these shameful atrocities. But Louis would not hear to any of the suggestions of these whisperers in his court. Instead they were amazed to see him preparing a list of all the names of men who had been guilty of crimes against himself. Behind each name, he was placing a red cross.

His enemies, hearing of this, were filled with dread alarm. They thought that the sign of a cross meant a sentence to death on the gallows. One after the other, they fled the court and their beloved country.

But King Louis learning of their flight called for a special session of the court to explain his list of names and the little red crosses.

"Be content, and do not fear," he said in a most cordial tone. "The cross which I drew by your names is not a sign of punishment, but a pledge of forgiveness and a seal for the sake of the crucified Saviour, who upon His cross forgave all His enemies, prayed for them, and blotted out the handwriting that was against them."

What about:

6. Our Sins: Are we to forget them? Can we forget them? Don't dig up the sins God has buried. If you have repented of them and asked forgiveness, don't be digging up that which God has buried. Don't be trying to bring before His face that which He has cast behind His back. Don't be trying to recall that which God hath forgotten. Don't be trying to bring up before you the things God has "washed white as snow." Don't be trying to write again that which God has blotted out. All manner of sin shall be forgiven unto men except the sin against the Holy Ghost (Matthew 12:31). "And they shall teach no more every man his neighbour, and every man his brother, saying, Know the LORD: for they shall all know me, from the least of them unto the greatest of them, saith the LORD: for I will forgive their iniquity, and I will remember their sin no more" (Jeremiah 31:34).

All the times you have forgotten Me, I will forget. Your frozen indifference, I will forget. Your years of sin and neglect, I will forget. Your fornication and uncleanness, I will forget. That is what God is saying—saying to you. Thy sins I will cast into the depths of the sea (Micah 7:19). Then—shall I be diving down to get them? Not unless I want to label myself a fool. "As far as the east is from the west, so far hath he removed our transgressions from us" (Psalms 103:12). Shall I be disturbed as to that distance? No. Then, shall I be inviting these sins to come back? No. I will abhor that which is evil henceforth and cleave to that which is good, and let the dead bury their dead. We should be found: "Giving thanks unto the Father, which hath made us meet to be partakers of the inheritance of the saints in light: Who hath delivered us from the power of darkness, and hath translated us into the kingdom of his dear Son: In whom we have redemption through his blood, even the forgiveness of sins: (Colossians 1:12–14).

He blots out of the book of His remembrance all our unholy living—IF. If what? If we will repent and turn again to God. God says: "Come now, and let us reason together, . . . though your sins be as scarlet, they shall be as white as snow; though they be red like crimson, they shall be as wool" (Isaiah 1:18). If we will trust only in Him who took our place, sin's place on the cross. ". . . God for Christ's sake hath forgiven you" (Ephesians 4:32). ". . . your sins are forgiven for his name's sake" (I John 2:12).

What comfort and gladness it should bring to our lives! Wherever God's light shines, God's truth shall shine; wherever God's heat glows, God's love shall glow; wherever God's wind breathes, God's spirit shall breathe; wherever God's water flows, God's salvation shall flow; wherever God's ground blooms, God's grace shall blossom; wherever God's ransomed sinners have wandered, God's white-robed saints shall find a home. Wherever sin has kindled a blush of shame, the tears of penitence shall glisten in the radiance of reconciliation. Wherever death has dropped the curtain around an evening sleeper, the angel of hope shall hand her lamp from the lintel, and sit down upon the threshold, beside the angel of the resurrection to wonder at the beauty of the night, and wait for the glory of the morning.

There is a day coming when all the perversion of true religion and all the devices of false religion shall surrender to One infinitely mightier than they. And the "faithful saying, worthy of all acceptation" shall win all acceptation. Then the flowery vales unblighted by crime, the golden mountains undarkened by wrath, the holy isles like recovered Edens, the happy continents like symbolic heavens—from sea to sea shall sing, from shore to shore shall ring, from the deepest depth shall cry, from the highest heights reply, and thrill the enchanted sky—with the only good news on earth, the gladdest glad tidings on earth, the gladdest glad tidings under heaven—"that Christ Jesus came into the world to save sinners"— and "through this man is preached unto us the forgiveness of sins."

Let us have—at this end of the year:

7. THE TODAY-TOMORROW MIND: The tomorrow mind—not in foolish boasting as to there being plenty of time. The tomorrow mind —not in impenitence as to sins, but in resolve to make life more sinless than ever before. The tomorrow mind—"forgetting the things of the past." The tomorrow mind—"looking unto Jesus." The mind of a great achiever is a tomorrow mind. The mind of a failure is a yesterday mind.

Which way is your face set? If it is toward the future, you are living in sunshine. If it is toward the past, you get doubt, cold, and fog. Life is filled with hard knocks. One man, after a blow, sits down and cries. The other type wipes the blood from his face and fights on. No rebuff can stay the indomitable soul. No triumph can stiffen the backbone of a whiner. There are women who never rise from their first bereavement. To them, loyalty means the eternal shadow. To bury the past appears to them cold and heartless. But they need to learn that the past exists as soil from which to grow the future. The past is the dead mold. The future is the living lily. Tomorrow is big with promise. Tomorrow is full of spirit ozone. Tomorrow is strong with intellectual dynamics. Tomorrow is rich in the elements of happiness.

"Let the dead bury their dead." To you who have deserted your ideals, there is a Land of Beginning Again. To you whose hearts, dried and cold, have killed love, there is a Land of Beginning Again. To you in whose bosoms are the serpents of self-contempt, seeking self-respect you longed for, begin again. To you who are world-weary rich—loathing yourselves and your possessions—begin again. To you who are the fools who sold your birthright for a mess of pottage, begin again. To you who are undisciplined, who have sacrificed all for a minute of anger or an hour of lust, begin again. To you who have taken the wrong fork of the road and found out your mistake too late, there is, by the grace of God, the Land of Beginning Again. To the painted woman whose heart is a sepulchre, go to that land. To the drug taker with brain afire, go to that land, that blessed Land of Beginning Again.

Let the dead bury their dead. Don't look back. Finish with the past. The past, be it good or be it bad, is all over. If you have done wrong, begin now to do right. If you have been dishonest, begin now to ". . . Provide things honest in the sight of all men" (Romans 12: 17). If you have been a "boozer" or a winebibber, begin now to be sober—remembering that "Wine is a mocker, strong drink is raging: and whosoever is deceived thereby is not wise" (Proverbs 20:1). If you have been unfair to yourself or to others, begin now to be fair and square with yourself, with others, with God. If you have inward griefs, take them out and bury them. Cleanse your heart of all bitterness. Start afresh now, without an hour's delay, with the sword of a noble purpose in your hand and high hopes in your heart. If you have grudges, treat them as you would deal with deadly mosquitos. If you have enmities and hates, shoo them away as filthy flies that spoil the fair and wholesome meats of life.

Doing these wise things, we shall be able to close and lock all doors on all yesterdays with their sorrows, their miserable mistakes, their failures, their heartaches, their defeats, their tears, their fears, their doubts, their glooms. Then, throwing the keys away, we can go forth to be ". . . steadfast, unmoveable, always abounding in the work of the Lord . . ."—knowing assuredly that our ". . labour is not in vain in the Lord" (I Corinthians 15:58).

V

Declared Directions

---

*...I bow my knees unto the Father of our Lord Jesus Christ
...that ye, being rooted and grounded in love, May be able to
comprehend with all saints ... the breadth, and length, and
depth, and height* (Ephesians 3:14, 17–18).

Paul, an apostle of Jesus Christ by the will of God (Ephesians
1:1), a prisoner of Jesus Christ for the Gentiles (Ephesians 3:1), a
servant of Jesus Christ (Philippians 1:1), a soldier of the cross who
endured hardness for Christ, who bore in his body the marks of the
Lord Jesus (Galatians 6:17), wrote to the church at Ephesus—to the
saints who were at Ephesus, and to the faithful in Christ Jesus
(Ephesians 1:1). In the third chapter of this epistle, he writes of how
God made him a preacher, saying: "... I was made a minister according to ... the grace of God given unto me by the effectual working of his power" (Ephesians 3:7),—"... that I should preach among
the Gentiles the unsearchable riches of Christ; and to make all men
see what is the fellowship of the mystery, which from the beginning
of the world hath been hid in God, who created all things by Jesus
Christ: To the intent that now unto the principalities and powers in
heavenly places might be known by the church the manifold wisdom
of God, According to the eternal purpose which he purposed in
Christ Jesus our Lord: In whom we have boldness and access with
confidence by the faith of Him" (Ephesians 3:8–12).

Paul, who practiced what he preached in urging people to pray
without ceasing by himself praying without ceasing, prayed that
Christ might dwell in the hearts of the Ephesians by faith—that they,

being rooted and grounded in love, "May be able to comprehend with all saints what is the breadth, and length, and depth, and height; And to know the love of Christ, which passeth knowledge, that ye might be filled with all the fulness of God" (Ephesians 3:18-19).

I beseech you now to pitch your mental tent soberly and heart-searchingly upon some truths that are suggested and that circle around the word "Length"—as we think of God's eternal purposes of grace through Christ our Saviour and Lord, and as we see how all Bible roads lead to the place called Calvary (Luke 23:33), even as all the streams of civilization flow from Calvary. Moreover, this word "Length" declares some directions we should note and emphasize.

Think of the:

1. FORWARD DIRECTION OF THE PROPHETIC ROAD: Long is that prophetic road. That road began in the garden of Eden where Adam, the federal head of the race, plunged into sin and carried the whole human race with him. ". . . by one man sin entered into the world, and death by sin; and so death passed upon all men, for that all have sinned" (Romans 5:12). ". . . by one man's offence death reigned by one . . . by the offence of one judgment came upon all men to condemnation; . . . by one man's disobedience many were made sinners, . . ." (Romans 5:17-19). There in the garden of Eden, where despair pitched his black pavillions upon man's sterile and blasted estate, began this long prophetic road which reached across the centuries—for there the Lord God spoke words of prophecy, saying: "And I will put enmity between thee and the woman, and between thy seed and her seed; it shall bruise thy head, and thou shalt bruise his heel" (Genesis 3:15).

On this prophetic road we see typical wonders. Adam is a figure of Christ. "Nevertheless death reigned from Adam to Moses, even over them that had not sinned after the similitude of Adam's transgression, who is the figure of him that was to come" (Romans 5:14).

Melchizedec is a figure of Christ.

> . . . Melchisedec, king of Salem, priest of the most high God, . . . Without father, without mother, without descent, having neither

beginning of days, nor end of life; but made like unto the Son of God . . . (Hebrews 7:1, 3).

Noah's Ark, with its one door, the only place where any living creature was safe from the destructive flood, pointed to Jesus who said, ". . . no man cometh unto the Father, but by me" (John 14:6).

Abraham, in whom the glories of the Hebrew race are summarized, on Mt. Moriah, after he had ". . . built an altar there, and laid the wood in order, and bound Isaac his son, and laid him on the altar upon the wood . . . stretched forth his hand, and took the knife to slay his son" (Genesis 22:9-10). Abraham is a type of the Father who ". . . spared not his own Son, but delivered him up for us all, . . ." (Romans 8:32). Isaac is a type of Christ ". . . obedient unto . . . the death of the cross" (Philippians 2:8). The ram caught in the thicket by his horns, which Abraham offered up for a burnt offering in the stead of his son (Genesis 22:13), is a type of substitution—of Christ offered as a burnt offering in our stead. "By the which will we are sanctified through the offering of the body of Jesus Christ once for all" (Hebrews 10:10).

Joseph, loved by Israel more than all his children—was the object of the malicious envy of his brethren (Genesis 37:3, 11) who conspired against him to slay him (Genesis 37:18), and was humiliated by being sold into slavery and later cast into Potiphar's prison—was a type of Christ, despised, abused, by wicked men. Then Joseph's exaltation, when Pharaoh ". . . took off his ring from his hand, and put it upon Joseph's hand, . . . and made him ruler over all the land of Egypt" (Genesis 41:42-43), was a type of Christ whom God hath highly exalted. While it is not asserted anywhere in the Bible that Joseph was a type of Christ, so many analogies are not accidents. Joseph was the special object of his father's love. So was Jesus. Joseph was hated by his brethren (Genesis 37:4). So was Jesus, hated without a cause (John 15:24-25). The rock which Moses struck in Horeb —the rock which when smitten gave forth water which the people drank (Genesis 17)—spoke of Christ.

Paul wrote: ". . . that Rock was Christ" (I Corinthians 10:4).

The manna which the children of Israel ate for forty years was a type of Christ, "the bread of life," come down from heaven to die for the life of the world (John 6:35, 48-51).

The first Tabernacle was a figure (or comparison) of Christ. ". . . the first tabernacle was . . . a figure for the time then present, in which were offered both gifts and sacrifices, . . ." (Hebrews 9:8-9).

Moses was a type of Christ—because he was a deliverer from bondage. Joshua was a type of Christ because he was a conqueror. Samson was a type of Christ because of his strength to slay the lions and carry off the gates of impossibility. Solomon was a type of Christ because of the affluance of his reign. Jonah was a type of Christ because of the stormy sea into which he threw himself for the rescue of others. The diversified and systematic sacrifices of the Jews were the shadows of redemptive entity still far ahead.

The lambs on Jewish altars slain pointed to the sacrifice of the Lamb of God slain—in the redemptive purposes of God, from before the foundation of the world, and actually by wicked hands, slain on Calvary.

The slaughter of oxen and sheep were adumbrations of a substance yet to come—causing the hymn writer Isaac Watts thinking upon their significance, to write:

> Not all the blood of beasts
> On Jewish altars slain,
> Could give the guilty conscience peace
> Or wash away the stain.
>
> But Christ, the heavenly Lamb
> Takes all our sins away—
> A sacrifice of nobler name
> And richer blood than they.

All the sacrifices of animals offered by the Jews were bloody fingers of prophecy pointing down the long road to Calvary. These sacrifices were elemental. They were preparatory. They were rudimental. They were introductory. They all pointed to Christ, the propellent center to which the faith of mankind, before and since, gravitated.

The prophetic promises made by God to fallen man in Eden mean Christ crucified. The ceremonies of Judaism, containing mysterious prophecies, mean Christ crucified. The music of Israel's sweetest prophetic harps means Christ crucified. The light that burns in many prophecies means Christ crucified. The serpent of brass which Moses made and set upon a pole, upon which serpent anyone bitten of snakes might look and be healed and live, is a type of Christ and points to Christ "made to be sin for us" (II Corinthians 5:21)— as Jesus said to Nicodemus: "And as Moses lifted up the serpent in the wilderness, even so must the Son of man be lifted up:" (John 3:14).

The Passover, with the lamb without blemish which was slain, pointed in the forward direction to Christ and Calvary's cross. God said: "For I will pass through the land of Egypt this night, and will smite all the firstborn in the land of Egypt, both man and beast; and against all the gods of Egypt I will execute judgment: I am the LORD. And the blood shall be to you for a token upon the houses where ye are: and when I see the blood, I will pass over you, and the plague shall not be upon you to destroy you, when I smite the land of Egypt" (Exodus 12:12–13). And, looking backward along that road when so many prophetic fingers pointed forward, Paul wrote: ". . . Christ our passover is sacrificed for us:" (I Corinthians 5:7). And Peter, thinking upon the Passover night which pointed to the night upon Calvary, thinking upon the Passover Lamb without blemish, wrote: ". . . ye know that ye were not redeemed with corruptible things, as silver and gold, . . . But with the precious blood of Christ, as of a lamb without blemish and without spot: . . . foreordained before the foundation of the world, . . ." (I Peter 1:18–20). All Bible types are so related to Christ that Christ alone explains them—and Jesus alone is the vital substance that gives meaning to the Bible's genealogies, its histories and chronologies.

Think now of the:

2. DOWNWARD DIRECTION OF THE HUMILIATION ROAD: Jesus spoke

of this direction downward when, answering His malicious critics, He said: ". . . Verily, verily, I say unto you, Moses gave you not that bread from heaven; but my Father giveth you the true bread from heaven. For the bread of God is he which cometh down from heaven, and giveth life unto the world" (John 6:32–33). Notice the downward direction when He said: "For I came down from heaven, . . ." (John 6:38). Again, He said: "And no man hath ascended up to heaven, but he that came down from heaven, even the Son of man which is in heaven" (John 3:13). Notice that word "down." And that wonderful elaboration Paul gives of that word and the descent of Jesus along the humiliation road when he wrote by the Holy Spirit:

> Let this mind be in you, which was also in Christ Jesus: Who, being in the form of God, thought it not robbery to be equal with God: But made himself of no reputation, and took upon him the form of a servant, and was made in the likeness of men: And being found in fashion as a man, he humbled himself, and became obedient unto death, even the death of the cross (Philippians 2:5–8).

And Paul points again to the descent of that humiliation road when he united the ascent after the crucifixion with the descent to the crucifixion:

> Now that he ascended, what is it but that he also descended first into the lower parts of the earth? He that descended is the same also that ascended up far above all heavens, that he might fill all things (Ephesians 4:9–10).

Isaiah, looking forward along the prophetic road, sets in striking words Christ's sufferings in His descent along the humiliation road:

> He is despised and rejected of men; a man of sorrows, and acquainted with grief: and we hid as it were our faces from him; he was despised, and we esteemed him not. Surely he hath borne our griefs, and carried our sorrows: yet we did esteem him stricken, smitten of God, and afflicted. But he was wounded for our transgressions, he was bruised for our iniquities: the chastisement of our peace was upon him; and with his stripes we are healed (Isaiah 53:3–5).

Not only so. The Gospel writers depict some of the abuses Christ endured in that humiliation road:

And the men that held Jesus mocked him, and smote him. And when they had blindfolded him, they struck him on the face, and asked him, saying, Prophesy, who is it that smote thee? And many other things blasphemously spake they against him (Luke 22:63-65).

Then the high priest rent his clothes, saying, He hath spoken blasphemy; what further need have we of witnesses? behold, now ye have heard his blasphemy. What think ye? They answered and said, He is guilty of death. Then did they spit in his face, and buffeted him; and other smote him with the palms of their hands, Saying, Prophesy unto us, thou Christ, Who is he that smote thee? (Matthew 26:65-68).

And some began to spit on him, and to cover his face, and to buffet him, and to say unto him, Prophesy: and the servants did strike him with the palms of their hands (Mark 14:65).

Then the soldiers of the governor took Jesus into the common hall, and gathered unto him the whole band of soldiers. And they stripped him, and put on him a scarlet robe. And when they had platted a crown of thorns, they put it upon his head, and a reed in his right hand: and they bowed the knee before him, and mocked him, saying, Hail, King of the Jews! And they spit upon him, and took the reed, and smote him on the head (Matthew 27:27-30).

Then Pilate therefore took Jesus, and scourged him. And the soldiers platted a crown of thorns, and put it on his head, and they put on him a purple robe, And said, Hail, King of the Jews! and they smote him with their hands (John 19:1-3).

And they smote him on the head with a reed, and did spit upon him, and bowing their knees worshipped him (Mark 15:19).

All of these abuses, pictured to us in words, show the downward direction of humiliation road when Jesus came "down from his glory." Jesus came down from the heights of deity to the depths of humanity. Jesus came down from the adorations of heaven to the animosities and abominations of earth, down from the blessedness of heaven to the bindings and buffetings and bruises of men's hands and fists, down from the coronations of heaven to the condemnation and curses of men, down from the delights of heaven to the defamations of earth, down from the excellencies of heaven to the execrations and executions of earth, down from the favor of the Father's face to the fury of men's faces, down from the glory place in heaven to the gory place on Golgotha, down from the happiness and hallelujahs of heaven to the hisses of those who hated him, down from the intercessions of heaven to the iniquitous injustices of earth, down from the joys of heaven to the jeers of earth, down from the kindness of heaven to the killings of earth, down from the love of heaven to the lying of wicked mouths, down from the majesty of heaven to the miseries of earth, down from the notables of heaven to the nothingness of earth where he made himself of no reputation, down from the overshadowings of heaven's love to the onus of the cross, down from the place of praise to the place of perfidy, down from the sweet quietness of heaven to the bitter quarrels of earth, down from the receptions and rejoicing of angelic hosts to the rejection and ribald ridicule of stupid multitudes, down from the singing of heaven to the sneers of earth, down from the throne of heaven to the tree on Calvary, down from the place where angels united to do him reverence to the place where men united to do him violence, down from the virtues of heaven's hosts to the vileness and the vituperation of the motley crowds, down from the worship of heaven's multitudes to the wrath of the wicked who ". . . reviled him, wagging their heads" (Matthew 27:39).

Who can describe the depths of degradation into which He went —traveling down the humiliation road?

Let us consider the:

3. INWARD DIRECTION OF THE AGONY ROAD: Isaiah, in whose preaching were the thunders and lightnings of Sinai and the foregleams of Calvary, pointed Him out as a sojourner on that inward road of agony in these words: "He is a man of sorrows and acquainted with grief," "He was oppressed and he was afflicted," "It pleased the Lord to bruise him," and "He shall see of the travail of his soul."

"The travail of his soul." There is the inward direction of the agony road. And Jesus said: ". . . My soul is exceeding sorrowful, even unto death: . . ." (Matthew 26:38). "And being in an agony he prayed more earnestly: and his sweat was as it were great drops of blood falling down to the ground" (Luke 22:44).

Yes, beginning that tragic night, "to be sore amazed and to be very heavy," Jesus saith unto the disciples, ". . . My soul is exceeding sorrowful unto death: . . ." (Mark 14:33-34). There, the weight of the cross was weighing more heavily on His heart than it did a few hours later on His shoulders. Thus we see that the soul of Jesus' suffering was the suffering of His soul.

Again. Speaking anticipatingly by the Spirit through the prophet Jeremiah, the Christ of God says: "Is it nothing to you, all ye that pass by? behold, and see if there be any sorrow like unto my sorrow, which is done unto me, wherewith the LORD hath afflicted me in the day of his fierce anger" (Lamentations 1:12). ". . . the comforter that should relieve my soul is far from me: . . ." (Lamentations 1:16). How appropriately applicable this statement is to Jesus on the agony road.

"From above he hath sent fire into my bones." Note the inward direction of that suffering. God sent down fire from above—the fire of God's wrath due us. That fire burned into the depths of His soul —burning inwardly more than outwardly. Soul agony was His when He said, ". . . shame hath covered my face" (Psalms 69:7). Soul agony was His when the Saviour prophetically said to the Father in the midst of His sorrow: ". . . the reproaches of them that reproached thee are fallen on me" (Psalms 69:9). Dr. S. Franklin Logsdon, commenting on that, said: "Note the word *fallen*. There was not a gradual imposition of maltreatment going successively from one stage to another with a slight increase of intensity in the development. Rather did it seem that all hell pounced upon God's humble Lamb with a sudden and sustained violence with no surcease until sin's lashing storm had spent its force utterly. It was a *falling* weight. The reproaches *fell* upon the Saviour." (From *Lingering at Calvary,* by permission of Evangelical Publishers, Toronto, Canada.)

Christ's soul suffering is set forth in these words: "Reproach hath broken my heart; . . ." (Psalms 69:20). What a toll He paid "at the gate to life eternal" in mental torture as well as physical suffering! We know that Jesus had a human nature and a divine nature. So human was He that He had to rest—and so divine He gave, and gives even now, rest to the weary who come to Him. So human was He that He had to sleep—and so divine that He arose from sleep and rebuked a raging sea into the quietness of a dog asleep at his master's feet. So human was He that He had to eat—and so divine that He fed thousands with a lad's lunch. So human was He that a ship carried Him—and so divine that He walked on the sea to rescue His disciples in their distress and fear. So human was He that He longed for human companionship and human sympathy—and so divine that He said, ". . . the Father hath not left me alone; . . ." (John 8:29). So human was He that He wept—and so divine that He stood at the grave where He wept and called the dead Lazarus back to life. And on this agony road going into the sacred precincts of His soul both the human and the divine nature in Christ suffered agony.

> But we see Jesus, who was made a little lower than the angels for the suffering of death, crowned with glory and honour; that he by the grace of God should taste death for every man (Hebrews 2:9).

And that tasting death was not only in the human realm. Years ago, a great and wise man placed as an invaluable treasure in my mind and heart the truth that, had it been no more than Christ's human nature which suffered, then Christ would have suffered only finite suffering—and that if only the human nature of Jesus suffered, and suffered only a short time, we cannot say His sufferings were infinite. Then if His sufferings were not infinite, they could not be a satisfaction for our sins which, in their soul-damning and soul-dooming power, demand infinite suffering. Moreover, as some great and wise scholars have said, if the divine nature did not suffer in its union with the human nature, then a suffering Saviour—with the beard plucked from His face of flesh, with the brow of flesh punctured with thorns, with His body bent and His hands and feet of flesh pierced with the crucifixion nails—is no revelation of the nature of God. Not only so. If, as I was taught to believe, only Jesus' human nature suffered, and that suffering was apart from the suffering of the divine nature, then we have an infinite debt of sin cancelled by finite suffering, which, despite any arguments to the contrary, is an absurdity bordering on idiocy. How can our salvation from bondage into liberty, from darkness unto light, from corruption unto consecration, from condemnation unto justification, from damnation to salvation, from death unto life, merit endless renown and be the theme of the song of the redeemed if only a *finite* price was paid? Jesus, by both physical and soul suffering, paid our sin debt in full. And there is no lack or insufficiency in the ransom price He paid. And, knowing that there is no weakness or insufficiency in His surety, we, saved by the blood of the crucified Christ, can say to Satan, to hell, to earth, to heaven:

> For I am persuaded, that neither death, nor life, nor angels, nor principalities, nor powers, nor things present, nor things to come, Nor height, nor depth, nor any other creature, shall be able to separate us from the love of God, which is in Christ Jesus our Lord (Romans 8:38–39).

We should think of the:

4. OUTWARD DIRECTION OF THE INVITATION ROAD: The direction of the invitation road is outward—to the North, the South, the East, the West—extending to all the corners of all the continents of earth.

This invitation is outward to all who are included in that immensely important word "Whosoever." It has been said that that word is general and particular—embracing all and touching each. As Nathan to David said, "Thou art the man," so God's invitation is to each individual in the mass of men. "Come now, and let us reason together, saith the LORD: though your sins be as scarlet, they shall be as white as snow; though they be red like crimson, they shall be as wool" (Isaiah 1:18). This invitation reaches as far as sin has reached. And since we know that no race and no individual is free from sin, so also do we know that the reach of this invitation is to every race and to every man of every race. Since all men everywhere are from first to last, guilty before God, since all are under sin and justly condemned to suffer the wrath of God which is revealed from heaven against all ungodliness and unrighteousness of men, so is God's invitation to all in bondage to come to Christ and receive liberty—to all in darkness to come to Christ and receive light—to all who are dead in trespasses and sins to come to Christ and receive life that shall endless be.

> In the last day, that great day of the feast, Jesus stood and cried, saying, If any man thirst, let him come unto me, and drink (John 7:37).

Since Christ died for all the invitation is to all.

> Again, he sent forth other servants, saying, Tell them which are bidden, Behold, I have prepared my dinner: my oxen and my fatlings are killed, and all things are ready: come unto the marriage.
> Go ye therefore into the highways, and as many as ye shall find, bid to the marriage (Matthew 22:4, 9).

Since Jesus tasted death for every man (Hebrews 2:9), since Jesus gave His life a ransom for all (I Timothy 2:6), since Jesus is the propitiation for our sins, and not for ours only, but for the sins of the whole world (I John 2:2), so this invitation goes in all directions to all peoples.

God is not willing that any should perish. This precious truth is authenticated by the words of Jesus:

> All that the Father giveth me shall come to me; and him that cometh to me I will in no wise cast out.
> And this is the will of him that sent me, that every one which seeth the Son, and believeth on him, may have everlasting life: and I will raise him up at the last day (John 6:37, 40).

The word "whosoever" means *all* men and *any* man—all are invited.

Once Aquinaldo, the rebel chief of the Philippine Islands, was at large and fighting against our nation. Long was the search for him —and many were the soldiers of our army who were sacrificed until he was at last captured. When taken to Manila, into the presence of the U.S. authorities, was he at once beheaded as mere justice would indicate? By no means. He was given the privilege of swearing allegiance to the United States and to receive all that might be granted to a citizen of this country. And this he accepted in place of banishment from his native land.

Wondrous story of mercy this, that the nation should spend so much money and sacrifice so many lives to catch the worst rebel, to bestow upon him pardon and the richest blessings. Yet this is only the story in faint outline of God's mercy to us. God has gone to infinite expense and the sacrifice of His Only Son that we might be presented with the richest blessings of heaven. "Him that cometh unto me I will in no wise cast out." Nobody can make a plea in our behalf because of our innocence.

At the treason trial of Alfred Dreyfus, Emile Zola said:

Dreyfus is innocent. I swear it! I stake my life on it—my honor! At this solemn moment, in the presence of this tribunal, which is the representative of human justice: before you, gentlemen, who are the very incarnation of the country, before the whole of France, before the whole world, I swear that Dreyfus is innocent. By my forty years of work, by the authority that this toil may have given me, I swear that Dreyfus is innocent. By the name I have made for myself, by my works which have helped for the expansion of French literature, I swear that Dreyfus is innocent. May all that melt away, may my works perish, if Dreyfus be not innocent! He is innocent. All seems against me—the two Chambers, the civil authority, the most widely-circulated journals, the public opinion which they have poisoned. And I am quite calm; I shall conquer. I have for me only the ideal— an ideal of truth and justice. I was determined that my country should not remain the victim of lies and injustice. I may be condemned here. The day will come when France will thank me for having helped to save her honor.

Nobody can know anything about us and claim that we are innocent. Each of us has to confess in these words, "I have sinned," even as Pharaoh and Achan, King Saul and the Prodigal did.

And the Spirit and the bride say, Come. And let him that heareth say, Come. And let him that is athirst come. And whosoever will, let him take the water of life freely (Revelation 22:17).

Whosoever!

Whosoever *believeth!*

Christ's constituency is limited to no bounds, to no limitations. His offer is *to* all classes, even as His death was *for* all classes. He offers to *save* all the masses, even as He died *for* the masses. "Whosoever" means all the old, all the youth of the world, the rich, the poor, "Whosoever" means the high and low, the educated and the ignorant. It is all inclusive. Wherever "that which was lost" exists—there is the Son of man "able, willing, mighty to save" all who believe in Him.

Finally, let us consider soberly the:

5. ALL-DIRECTION OF THE SERVICE ROAD: "The field is the world." Men are not recipients of God's grace to sleep, but to serve. Men are not saved to sit, but to serve. Men are not brought from death unto life to use life selfishly, but to lessen the sum of human anguish. Only as we serve do we weigh creditably on God's scales. Only as we do with our might what our hands find to do to lessen the sum of human anguish and make real to many the joy that is ever rich and abiding, do we reach the spiritual stature which is well-pleasing unto God.

This service road goes North, South, East, West. There is no place our eyes can see, no place where human voices are heard, no place where human footprints are found, no place where human hands toil, no place where human language is uttered, no place where human hearts ache, but there are opportunities for service—opportunities available for us so to live that God may be glorified in us as the sun is glorified in rare and fragrant and beautiful flowers. For us Jesus came down from the heights of deity to the depths of humanity. Should any distance be too great for us to go for Him?

For us, Jesus walked the rough road blocked at the end with a bloody Roman cross. Should any road be too rough for us to travel for Jesus?

For us, Jesus bore a cross so heavy He fell beneath its crushing weight. Should any load be too heavy for us to carry for Jesus?

For our welfare, Jesus was known as "a man of sorrows and acquainted with grief." Should any sorrow be too severe for us to endure for Jesus?

For us, Jesus was reviled and abused and cruelly criticised and falsely accused. Should any malicious criticism and evil misunderstanding be too hard for us to suffer for Jesus?

For us, Jesus was assaulted by and fought with Satan. Should any battle be too sore and too long for us to fight—as we "endure hardness as good soldiers of the Cross of Christ"?

Someone said: "I should have been proud to have held the spyglass for Columbus, to have picked up his fallen brush for Michael Angelo, to have carried Milton's bag, to have blacked Shakespeare's boots, to have blown the bellows for Handel."

Greater than all things thus mentioned and as great as the greatest things that men have ever done for God can we do "as unto Christ."

> And whatsoever ye do in word or deed, do all in the name of the Lord Jesus, giving thanks to God and the Father by him (Colossians 3:17).

> And whatsoever ye do, do it heartily, as to the Lord, and not unto men; knowing that of the Lord ye shall receive the reward of the inheritance: for ye serve the Lord Christ (Colossians 3:23–24).

Let us travel this service road—this all-direction road—with a seven-fold consecration, knowing that our eyes are to be upon Jesus: "Looking unto Jesus the author and finisher of our faith; who for the joy that was set before him endured the cross, despising the shame, and is set down at the right hand of the throne of God" (Hebrews 12:2). And knowing, too, that our feet are to be in the race:

> Wherefore seeing we also are compassed about with so great a cloud of witnesses, let us lay aside every weight, and the sin which doth so easily beset us, and let us run with patience the race that is set before us (Hebrews 12:1).

And knowing also that our hands are to minister to others: "Let him that stole steal no more: but rather let him labour, working with his hands the thing which is good, that he may have to give to him that needeth" (Ephesians 4:28).

Knowing all the time that our minds are to be set on things

above: "Set your affection on things above, not on things on the earth" (Colossians 3:2). Knowing, by night and by day, that our hearts are to be established in grace, let us

> Be not carried about with divers and strange doctrines. For it is a good thing that the heart be established with grace; not with meats, which have not profited them that have been occupied therein (Hebrews 13:9).

And knowing, moreover, that our bodies are to be daily a living sacrifice:

> I beseech you therefore, brethren, by the mercies of God, that ye present your bodies a living sacrifice, holy, acceptable unto God, which is your reasonable service (Romans 12:1).

Yea, verily, ourselves—spirit, soul, body—blameless at the coming of our Lord Jesus:

> And the very God of peace sanctify you wholly; and I pray God your whole spirit and soul and body be preserved blameless unto the coming of our Lord Jesus Christ (I Thessalonians 5:23).

VI

Great Is the Lord

Great is the Lord, and greatly to be praised ...
... this God is our God for ever and ever; he will be our guide
even unto death   (Psalms 48:1, 14).

As we think upon God's greatness—calling for great praise, let us
consider the solemn:

1. Axiomatic Assertions:

"God is."

"Thou art."

"In the beginning God ..." (Genesis 1:1).

Through Hosea, the prophet, God said: "... I am God, and not
man; ..." (Hosea 11:9).

Like many stars glowing like white pearls on blue velvet, like
many flowers painted and fringed with God's glory, like crystal
streams threading a vast continent, like the heavens which declare
the glory of God and burn man's insignificance into man, are the
superb statements that abash us with their mightiness: "God is,"
"Thou art," "I am the Lord," "I am God."

God is the Creator behind all creation. God is the Designer behind all design. God is the Lawmaker behind all law. God is the
supreme fact of history. God is the supreme fact of science. God is the
supreme fact of philosophy. God is the supreme fact of personal life.
God is the supreme fact of life, of death, of Time, of Eternity. God is
the Mighty God personally and actively present in the affairs of the
universe. God is the great need of the human heart. God is the great

need of all true philosophy. God is the great need of the vast creation in which we live. And only "The fool hath said in his heart, There is no God . . ." (Psalms 14:1). A creation with no God! Who can conceive of such a thing? Given the creature—and the Creator is an axiom. There can not be a here without a there. There can not be an after without a before. There can never be an upper without a lower, a creature without the Creator, thought without a thinker, action without an actor, a book without an author. There can be no love without a person who loves. Such realities are all axioms—all self-evident. These things just mentioned all go together. Nothing is builded without an architect and a builder. There is no watch without a watchmaker. The construction of a cathedral or of a world demands the mind of a designer and the power to design.

Heathenish and insane is the theory that the worlds and all things in all worlds—the constellations upon constellations, the cluster of the Pleiades, the unloosable bands of Orion, the Mazzaroth led forth in their season—are just the result of a fortuitous concourse of atoms. Paganistic and idiotic the fantastic theory of modern atheism—the theory that this and all other worlds are the result of "the accidental jostling of protons and electrons and evolved by chemical combinations from star dust." I stand with Lord Bacon, who said: "I had rather believe all the fables in legend and the Talmud and the Alcoran than that this universal frame is without a mind."

A young man, seeking to darken my counsel by words without wisdom, said: "I do not believe anything any more; I am an infidel and proud of it." I told this conceited youth that he was like the man who bragged about being cross-eyed, or the man who boasted of having a club foot, or the man who was proud of paralyzed muscles, or the man who rejoiced in being able to mumble the incoherency of idiocy. Then I told him that, despite his denials of belief, he was a very definite believer—because a man can not disbelieve without believing that he disbelieves. What must the unbeliever believe? That Providence is an idle dream, that prayer is a useless exercise, that heaven is a vain hope, that life is without inspiration, that death is without anticipation, that sorrow is without balm, that conscience is without authority, that sin is without accountability. Such is the belief of an infidel's unbelief.

God is—the great Unique and Unlike eternally. God is—and whoever exists without the knowledge of God is a wandering star, centerless and orbitless, reserved unto blackness and darkness forever. No wise person argues the existence of God. The Bible does not do it. The Bible takes God for granted. The Bible introduces us at once to His works. This is what we should do. It is hard for me to believe that any man at the center of his soul is an atheist. He is an atheist only at the surface of his critical judgment, an atheist only on the tip of his flippant tongue.

Now, considering God's greatness, think upon some of God's:

2. AFFIRMED ATTRIBUTES: God is eternal. God is the great I AM. With Moses we say:

> Lord, thou hast been our dwelling place in all generations. Before the mountains were brought forth, or ever thou hadst formed the earth and the world, even from everlasting to everlasting, thou art God (Psalms 90:1-2).

In God's sight, a thousand years are as one day—". . . as yesterday when it is passed, and as a watch in the night" (Psalms 90:4). The weight of such a ponderous thought makes the mind stagger. The imagination fails to cross the chasm of eternal years. All measures of time and space, and the powers of numbers are reduced to meaningless words when applied to the lifetime of God. The eternity of God forces us to clothe Him with an excellency of nature surpassing all other existences. The eternity of God removes Him infinitely beyond and above all other beings, with Calvary's cross a goal in His heart from all eternity. God inhabiteth eternity.

God is free. In the Sacred Record, he stands out untrammeled, unbound in the vast eternity from which he spoke a world into existence. The Universe is not the manifestation of a blind, non-thinking, non-willing, inexorable fate, that moves on without thought, without choice, without purpose to some unforeseen, yet inevitable end.

God is intelligent. Bible revelation and revelations in nature set
Him forth as the author of a universal order of matter, life, and mind
—such an order as could come only from a mind of infinite intelligence.

For my thoughts are not your thoughts, neither are your ways my
ways, saith the Lord. For as the heavens are higher than the earth, so
are my ways higher than your ways, and my thoughts than your
thoughts (Isaiah 55:8–9).

God is holy. The Psalmist speaks of God as "the high and holy
One." The Psalmist says: "The Lord is . . . holy in all his works"
(Psalms 145:17). The seraphim of Isaiah cried one to another and
said: ". . . Holy, holy, holy, is the Lord of hosts: . . ." (Isaiah 6:3).

In the Apocalypse, the living creatures around the throne cry:
". . . Holy, holy, holy, Lord God Almighty, which was, and is, and
is to come" (Revelation 4:8).

Isaiah records these words of God:

For thus saith the high and lofty One that inhabiteth eternity, whose
name is Holy; I dwell in the high and holy place, with him also that
is of a contrite and humble spirit, to revive the spirit of the humble,
and to revive the heart of the contrite ones (Isaiah 57:15).

Jesus taught that God is holy—and the only holy One. He
prayed, ". . . Holy Father, keep through thine own name those whom
thou hast given me, . . ." (John 17:11).

God is wise. Paul could not declare his conception of the wisdom
of God, and found it necessary to resort to exclamation. "O the depth
. . . both of the wisdom and knowledge of God! how unsearchable are
his judgments, and his ways past finding out!" (Romans 11:33).

God is Love. "He that loveth not knoweth not God; for God is
love. In this was manifested the love of God toward us, because that
God sent his only begotten Son into the world, that we might live
through him. Herein is love, not that we loved God, but that he
loved us and sent his Son to be the propitiation for our sins" (I John
4:8–10).

God is good. "The LORD is good to all: . . ." (Psalms 145:9). "O taste and see that the Lord is good: . . ." (Psalms 34:8).

Paul speaks of ". . . the riches of his goodness . . ." (Romans 2:4). David speaks of the earth being full of the goodness of the Lord (Psalms 33:5), of how God crowns the year with his goodness (Psalms 64:11), and of how men shall abundantly utter the memory of God's great goodness (Psalms 145:7).

God is merciful. God said: "I . . . will shew mercy on whom I will shew mercy" (Exodus 33:19). David said: ". . . I trust in the mercy of God . . ." (Psalms 52:8). ". . . Thy mercy is great above the heavens . . ." (Psalms 108:4). Paul said: "I beseech you . . . by the mercies of God, . . ." (Romans 12:1). Peter speaks of ". . . his abundant mercy . . ." (I Peter 1:3).

God is just. Paul speaks of God's righteousness—". . . that he might be just, and the justifier of him which believeth in Jesus" (Romans 3:26).

Peter, by the Holy Spirit, wrote: "For Christ also hath once suffered for sins, the just for the unjust, that he might bring us to God, . . ." (I Peter 3:18).

In thousands of ways and words, the Bible declares the truth that God is a God of truth and without iniquity, just and right.

God is omnipotent. To Abraham He said, "I am God Almighty." Still He holds this world in the hand of His omnipotence.

Of Him this is eternally true:

"Behold, the Lord God . . . Who hath measured the waters in the hollow of his hand, and meted out heaven with a span, and comprehended the dust of the earth in a measure, and weighed the mountains in scales, and the hills in a balance?" (Isaiah 40:10, 12).

Behold, the nations are as a drop of a bucket, and are counted as the small dust of the balance: behold, he taketh up the isles as a very little thing (Isaiah 40:15).

God is omniscient. "Neither is there any creature that is not manifest in his sight: but all things are naked and opened unto the eyes of him with whom we have to do" (Hebrews 4:13). "Yea, the darkness hideth not from thee; but the night shineth as the day: the darkness and the light are both alike to thee" (Psalms 139:12).

God is omnipresent. ". . . Whither shall I flee from thy presence? If I ascend up into heaven, thou art there: if I make my bed in hell, behold, thou art there. If I take the wings of the morning, and dwell in the uttermost parts of the sea; Even there shall thy hand lead me, and thy right hand shall hold me" (Psalms 139:7–10). "Doth not he see my ways, and count all my steps?" (Job 31:4). God fills heaven and earth. ". . . In him we live, and move, and have our being, . . ." (Acts 17:28).

Recognizing our frailty in comparison with His might, let us consider God's:

3. ASTONISHING ACTS: "Praise him for his mighty acts: . . ." (Psalms 150:2). "One generation shall praise thy works to another, and shall declare thy mighty acts" (Psalms 145:4). "He made known his ways unto Moses, his acts unto the children of Israel" (Psalms 103:7). "Who can utter the mighty acts of the LORD? who can shew forth all his praise?" (Psalms 106:2). "Now therefore stand still, that I may reason with you before the LORD of all the righteous acts of the LORD, which he did to you and to your fathers" (I Samuel 12:7). "But your eyes have seen all the great acts of the LORD which he did" (Deuteronomy 11:7). "And his miracles, and his acts, which he did in the midst of Egypt unto Pharaoh the king of Egypt, and unto all his land;" (Deuteronomy 11:3). "They that are delivered from the noise of archers in the places of drawing water, there shall they rehearse the righteous acts of the LORD, even the righteous acts toward the inhabitants of his villages in Israel: then shall the people of the LORD go down to the gates" (Judges 5:11).

O give thanks unto the Lord . . . who alone doeth great wonders. Give thanks unto the Lord—to him who smote Egypt in their first born, and brought Israel out from among the Egyptians, with a strong hand and a stretched-out arm, dividing the Red Sea into parts and making Israel to pass through the midst of it, but overthrew Pharaoh and his host in the Red Sea—and led his people through the wilderness (Psalms 136).

What astonishing acts of God we think upon when we read how God brought the Israelites out of darkness and the shadow of death, when they were bound in affliction and irons, and brake their bands asunder. "For he hath broken the gates of brass, and cut the bars of iron in sunder" (Psalms 107:16). He ". . . setteth . . . the poor on high from affliction, . . ." (Psalms 107:41). Think of the astonishing acts of God set forth in these words:

> And Moses called unto all Israel, and said unto them, Ye have seen all that the LORD did before your eyes in the land of Egypt unto Pharaoh, and unto all his servants, and unto all his land;
> And I have led you forty years in the wilderness: your clothes are not waxen old upon you, and thy shoe is not waxen old upon thy foot. Ye have not eaten bread, neither have ye drunk wine or strong drink: that ye might know that I am the LORD your God (Deuteronomy 29:2, 5–6).

> And thou didst divide the sea before them, so that they went through the midst of the sea on the dry land; and their persecutors thou threwest into the deeps, as a stone into the mighty waters. Moreover thou leddest them in the day by a cloudy pillar; and in the night by a pillar of fire, to give them light in the way wherein they should go. Thou camest down also upon Mount Sinai, and spakest with them from heaven, and gavest them right judgments, and true laws, good statutes and commandments: and madest known unto them thy holy sabbath, and commandedst them precepts, statutes, and laws, by the hand of Moses thy servant: And gavest them bread from heaven for their hunger, and broughtest forth water for them out of the rock for their thirst, and promisedst them that they should go in to possess the land which thou hadst sworn to give them (Nehemiah 9:11–15).

Think of our great God's astonishing acts manifest in the *magnificent*. "Thou art the God that doest wonders: . . ." (Psalms 77:14). "The heavens declare the glory of God; and the firmament sheweth his handywork" (Psalms 19:1).

God's great power in nature is magnificent. For example, the Victoria Falls of the Zambesi River are five times as great as Niagara. Above the falls, the river is two miles wide, narrowing to a mile when it makes the plunge of four hundred feet. The falls of Niagara have only seven million horse power, but the Victoria Falls have thirty-five million horse power. This power, if utilized, would equal one million tons per day.

See God's acts of magnificence in the planets, comets, and the sun in its tabernacle in the heavens, lighting up the worlds so far away—with its exhaustless energies of light and heat. Think of the system of worlds, infinite by every standard of measurement, spinning their way through the skies at amazing and exact speed, for ages maintaining their own meticulous orbits—no stop and go signs, no traffic cops, no collisions.

Look up at night. See the stars lying like diamonds on the black velvet of the darkness. "These are but dewdrops on the lawn of the Father's house." See the sun—ninety-three million miles away. It is but a porch lamp on the house not made with hands. President John Quincy Adams said that a study of the starry sky seems to lead man "blindfolded up to the council chambers of Omnipotence and there, stripping the bandage from their eyes, bid him look undazzled at the throne of God." The Milky Way is so big that it would take light one hundred million years to travel from one end of it to the other.

O the measureless and magnificent immensity of the skies! If our sun were hollow, it would be large enough to hold 1,400,000 worlds like this. The sun is a ball of fire. Its flames flash out three hundred thousand miles. It is estimated that the sun is so hot that if the earth were thrown into the sun it would burn up completely in one minute. Yet our sun is one of the smallest balls of fire in the universe. The nearest sun to ours is Alpha Centauri. It is twenty-five trillion, three hundred billions of miles away or 275,000 times as far away as is our sun from us. The size of some of these suns is staggering. In an issue of the American Magazine, published during the spring of 1923, was a description of the newly-discovered and one of the largest known suns. Betelgeuse is the name given to this star. It is 260 million miles in diameter. The diameter of Betelgeuse is more than three times the distance between the earth and its sun. That distance is 92 million miles while the sheer diameter of Betelgeuse is 260 million miles.

If an airplane had been used in Old Testament times and one of the machines had started from the earth to the planet Neptune via Mars, Jupiter, Saturn, and Uranus, in a regular non-stop flight in the days of the Judges (1170 B.C.) near the time of Jepthah (11th chapter), and traveled all the way at the rate of one hundred miles per hour, day and night, or twenty-four hundred miles per day, it would make the first lap of the journey from the earth to Mars (48,500,000 miles) in fifty-five years (1115 B.C.) at the death of Samson. The second lap of the journey from Mars to Jupiter (342,000,000 miles) would require 399 years. It passed Jupiter in 725 B.C., four years before Shalmanezer carried the ten tribes into captivity. The third lap of the journey would require 460 years and would pass Saturn in 265 B.C.

If the earth were as large as the sun and everything on it were as large in proportion, an object weighing one hundred pounds would weigh 2,760 pounds. A man six feet tall would be one-eighth of a mile high; his arms from shoulder to finger tips would be 160 feet long and his legs would be over 250 feet long. His eyes would be nine feet in diameter and his nose would be fourteen feet long. The ears would look like a wagon sheet half mast and the hair would look like a haystack. A common pin would be a column of brass and a lead pencil would be as large as an oak. The Mississippi River would be 140,000 miles long and 109 miles wide at Memphis, Tennessee.

Look at the constellation of Orion. More than six hundred light years from us, its vastness is beyond the power of words to describe. Astronomers tell us that from the center of the Orion Nebula the glory reaches out some trillion miles in all directions, for the diameter is about four light-years.

"Canst thou guide Arcturus with his sons?" Thus asked Job. No man can because this blazing sun, twenty-two times larger than our sun, moves through space like a rocket—gliding forward at over five thousand miles a minute—guided by its Creator.

The Palomar Observatory's two hundred-inch Hale telescope, largest in the world, has brought to view facts David never dreamed

of. It captures light that has been on its way to earth from the farthest
faint star for two billion years.

In astonishment and awe we say, with David:

> Who is like unto the LORD our God, who dwelleth on high, Who
> humbleth himself to behold the things that are in heaven, and in the
> earth! (Psalms 113:5-6).

See God acting astonishingly in the high mountains which are
oft cloaked with clouds and capped with diadems of snow, in the
mighty leaping waterfalls flinging themselves with the voice of
thunder from the heights, in the vast areas of coal, which are but the
sun's blood turned black.

See God acting astonishingly in the mighty oceans—rolling and
heaving, bearing the ships of the nations of earth.

See God manifesting Himself in magnificence in the millions of
worlds, each with its separate orbit, all balanced so wonderfully in
space. See God in magnificent manifestation in the grass, herbs, fruit-
bearing trees, and forests that carpet the earth with loveliness and in
the fishes of the seas and the winged fowls of the air. Think of His
magnificently astonishing acts in all the intricate and exact operations of Nature and in the ninety-two elements which constitute all
kinds of matter, from hydrogen at one end of the scale to uranium
at the other.

Think, too, of how God's astonishing acts are set forth in the
miniature.

Mighty is God when He works in miniature! A particle of radi-
um, so small we have to see it through a microscope to observe its
constituence, is so powerful it will ring a bell for thirty thousand
years. A crystalline protein molecule from the juice of diseased matter
consists of two million atoms.

Think of God and the diminutive mission. Think of the bee and
its work. A red clover blossom contains less than one-eighth of a
grain of sugar. Seven thousand grains are required to make a pound
of honey. A bee, flitting here and there for sweetness, must visit
56,000 clover heads for a pound of honey; and there are about sixty

flower heads to each clover head. When a bee performs that opera-
tion sixty by 56,000 times or 3,360,000 times, it secures sweetness
enough for only one pound of honey.

Think of the miniature marvels of the structure of bees and the
intricacy of their mysterious operations. The bee has three pairs of
legs. The nose of the bee has two or three thousand tiny sense plates.
The bee's wings beat 190 times a second, or 11,400 times a minute.

Think, too, of the ruby-throated humming bird—the only bird
that hibernates at night. So beautiful are the colors of these little birds
that Audubon has called them "glittering fragments of the rainbow."
These humming birds are the only land birds that can reverse their
wing action, moving backwards and forwards. Their wings move
so rapidly that one can see them only in a blur. They vibrate over
two hundred times per second—which is five or six times as fast as
an airplane propeller usually travels. Because of this, these birds can
appear to stand still in midair, or can support themselves while they
dip their beaks into a flower for nectar. They travel at fast speed—
one hundred feet per second, more than a mile a minute. God works
in the small, just as he marks the sparrow's fall.

An atom is said to be one million times smaller than the breadth
of a hair. Armed with the most powerful microscopes, only a few
have ever seen an atom. Yet the foundations of the universe are built
of atomic bricks or electronic grains of sand—if you desire a sugges-
tion of overwhelming infinitesimal proportions. "For if a molecule
is a microscopic house of which atoms are the bricks, is not an atom
a super-microscopic house of which electrons are the invisible atoms?"

God's astonishing acts manifest in miniature—in the diminutive
—just as He numbers the hairs of our heads, counts our footsteps,
knows our down-sitting and uprising, keeping acquainted with all of
our ways at all times and in all places.

Think reverently now of God's astonishing acts manifest in
mystery. Man can send an electric current through a copper wire at
sixty degrees below zero, and at the other end of the wire, heat a
platinum wire to one thousand degrees. Where was that heat? From
whence did it come? God—working in mystery!

Man drops mercury into naphthalene and changes it into phthalic acid. How can such be? God acting in mystery!

Man takes seven-tenths of one percent chromium and puts it into low-carbon steel and increases the tensile strength from 55,000 pounds to the square inch to 100,000 pounds to the square inch. God acting in mystery!

A storage battery weighing fifty pounds, fully charged, will do work in lifting one hundred pounds until its "soul" has been discharged. Still the battery has lost none of its fifty pounds. Why and how? God acting in mystery.

In the atomic nucleus of uranium there are said to be ninety-two protons and 146 neutrons with ninety-two out-reaching electrons. God acting in mystery.

The wax bees make floats on water and is strongly resistant to heat—enduring a temperature of 140 degrees Fahrenheit before melting. No other wax has such a high melting point. The reason for this is easily discernible. The entire store of honey would be lost if thin-walled treasure vaults, the storage chambers, softened under the influence of moderate heat and gave way. God working in mystery.

The magnet known as an "Alnico C-type Magnet," to distinguish it from the common iron horseshoe type, derives its name from the metals from which it is made—aluminum, nickel, and cobalt. C-type means shaped like a "C." Alnico magnets are made from these three metals which, singly, exhibit low magnetic properties, but when alloyed (fused) together produce the most powerful metallic magnet known. They are also the most permanent and most highly resistant to both shock and extreme temperatures. Everyone is familiar with aluminum and nickel. Cobalt is similar to nickel in appearance, but is harder and costlier. When alloyed with steel, an extremely hard, resistant metal is produced which is used in machinery to withstand abrasion, and in electric heating elements to withstand high temperatures and corrosion. God working in mystery.

Black carbon and colorless oxygen are both tasteless. Hydrogen is a colorless, tasteless, odorless gas, fourteen and one-half times lighter than an equal volume of air and 11,160 times lighter than water. We combine this hydrogen with black carbon and oxygen and get sweet white sugar. God working in mystery.

Think of the neutrino—an unbelievably tiny part of a cosmic ray particle. It has such great energy it could drive through solid lead two hundred quadrillion miles. God working in mystery.

The chemical laws which compel certain elements to combine according to atomic weights, and the law of multiple proportions, show the infinite wisdom of the Creator. Each atom of matter is stamped with laws that are definite and invariable so that it acts with absolute precision in all that it does, e.g., thirty-two pounds of sulphur must have fifty-six pounds of iron with which to unite—no more, no less. And so with all the elements. God acting in mystery.

The chemist marries oxygen and carbon, and the result of this chemical matrimony is flame. God acting in mystery.

Chemists have obtained two hundred by-products from coal tar. Nine hundred dyes in five thousand shades have been made from black carbon tar. The perfumes with which our wives and daughters dainty themselves and the aspirin which they take for headaches, come from the same source. Stranger still is the fact that quinine and saccharine, one bitterer than gall, the other sweeter than sugar, live side by side in the same old tar barrel. God acting in mystery!

Take toluene, a coal tar distillate. It smells like gasoline. Combine it with chlorine, one of the poisonous gases used in the war, and by treating it with another deadly poison, cyanide, we get a wonderful-smelling, non-poisonous, health-aiding substance which is a harmless medicine for children. God acting in mystery.

Water weighs eight hundred times more than air, yet, to have rain, it must be lifted against the force of gravity, held in suspension above the earth, moved to definite locations, and brought down as rain. It has been estimated that approximately sixteen million tons of water fall every second. Obviously this must have been raised from oceans and lakes and rivers to make its fall possible. God acting in mystery.

Snow descends from the great laboratory of the firmament. God working in mystery.

Ken Anderson asks us to think of the migratory flights of birds —the feathered and vocal flowers of the forest and field. When winter approaches, plumed caravans set out for the South. The bobolinks leaving in July, flutter through South Carolina in August, are in Cuba in September, and later go down over the Andes, and across Brazil to the marshlands of the Paraguay River.

The tiny blackpoll warblers go as far as five thousand miles, while night hawks of the Yukon region journey to Argentina. The golden plovers of Alaska span the two thousand miles between these and Hawaii without one stop-over! God working in mystery.

The Canadian humming bird, displaying the superiority of brain over brawn, nestles in the soft, warm feathers of the south-bound Canadian geese. Hunters, who have shot down the geese, have seen the little creatures dart away before their air-liner crashed.

How do these frail and feathered migrants find their way over long stretches without chart or compass? How is it that they, as Anderson asks, can be marked and thus know to return on subsequent summers to the same cluster of trees? What enables them to find their way unerringly through wind and rain along uncharted courses?

God working in mystery—as the One who made the birds and took time to teach them.

Looking up to the universe, with its billions of stars and millions of light years—looking down into the depths, scaling the heights, delving into the bosom and bowels of the earth, we exultantly and worshipfully exclaim with the Psalmist:

> Great is the LORD, and greatly to be praised; and his greatness is unsearchable. One generation shall praise thy works to another, and shall declare thy mighty acts. I will speak of the glorious honour of thy majesty, and of thy wondrous works (Psalms 145:3–5).

> He telleth the number of the stars; he calleth them all by their names. Great is our Lord, and of great power: his understanding is infinite. (Psalms 147:4–5).

> Which maketh Arcturus, Orion, and Pleiades, and the chambers of the south; Which doeth great things past finding out; yea, and wonders without number (Job 9:9–10).

Not only so. Let us think of this great God in:

4. AVAILABLE ACTUALITY: There came a time when this mighty God who manifests Himself in the magnificent, in miniature, and in mystery was manifest in the flesh (I Timothy 3:16). When was that? When Jesus came down from the heights of deity to the depths of humanity. John speaks of that available manifestation.

> That which was from the beginning, which we have heard, which we have seen with our eyes, which we have looked upon, and our hands have handled, of the Word of life; (For the life was manifested, and we have seen it, and bear witness, and shew unto you that eternal life, which was with the Father, and was manifested unto us;) (I John 1:1-2).

And when Christ was born, a world crisis was at its zenith. Only a faint throb in its heart testified that the world still lived. The scepter was frozen with the tyranny of impeached civilizations. As John B. Koehne tells us, the Jewish race slept, folded in robes of beautiful prophecy. Rome lay still, hushed by the terrible music of a tyrant's voice. Athens, the world's intellectual center, was drunk with the wine of skepticism. Egypt pillowed her head in the lap of the Sphinx. India, in the purpled East, dreamed of Buddha. China, crouched by her side, slept and, in her waking hours, gazed worshipfully upon ancestral tombs. Persia wore upon her brow a funeral wreath. "On that hard pagan world disgust and secret loathing fell, deaf weariness and sated lust made human life a hell."

Then God came in the flesh in the person of Jesus Christ. And Jesus who was from everlasting, the Ancient of Days, became the infant of days—a baby as old as His heavenly Father and ages older than His earthly mother. Jesus who "made all things" in creation was "made flesh" in incarnation, and bent the date lines of all nations around His manger cradle. Jesus who made man was made in the likeness of man. Jesus who created angels was made "a little lower than the angels." Jesus who was before Abraham, was born two thousand years after Abraham. Jesus who was David's son was David's Lord. Jesus who carried a nation out of Egypt was carried as a babe down into Egypt. Jesus who made all flesh was "made flesh." That day He was made flesh when a Jewish virgin who had never known a man travelled the travail road into that mysterious land of motherhood and came back holding in her arms the only baby who never had an earthly father. And His every muscle was a pulley divinely swung. His every nerve was divine handwriting, His every bone divine sculpture, His every heartbeat divine pulsation, His every breath divine whisper, His every cry God with no language but a cry.

John Milton had it right when he wrote:

> That glorious form, that Light unsufferable,
> That far-beaming blaze of majesty,
> Wherewith he wont at heaven's high council table
> To sit the midst of Tribal unity,
> He laid aside; and here, with us to be,
> Forsook the courts of everlasting Day—
> And chose with us a darksome house of clay.
>   (*The Morning of Christ's Nativity*)

"No man hath seen God at any time; the only begotten Son, which is in the bosom of the Father, he hath declared him" (John 1:18).

Paul spoke of Jesus as ". . . the image of the invisible God, the firstborn of every creature:" (Colossians 1:15).

"Jesus saith unto him, Have I been so long time with you, and yet hast thou not known me, Philip? he that hath seen me hath seen the Father; and how sayest thou then, Shew us the Father?" (John 14:9).

This shows that Jesus was infinite, for nothing less than infinity can reveal God. Whosoever reveals God must be God. Jesus expressed the entire being of God with entire precision, finality and perfection. In Him the silence of God breaks into full voice; without Him, the revealer of God, as Saviour and Lord, man is a failure, the world is a carcass, eternity is a vast horror. So Jesus in His character reveals God—exegetes God. To know Jesus is to know God. What Jesus was to prodigal and publican, to mother and child, to harlot and hypocrite, to saint and sinner, to rich and poor, to devils and disciples, that is God always, everywhere, to all people.

I once heard the late Dr. Robert L. Moyer say in a sermon:

In Jesus divine omnipotence moved in a human arm;
In Jesus divine wisdom was cradled in a human brain;
In Jesus divine love throbbed in a human heart;
In Jesus divine compassion glistened in a human eye;
In Jesus divine grace poured forth in human lips.

As the Father gazed into the eyes and inmost soul of His beloved Son, He saw every lineament of His own perfect Self, dwelling in measureless fullness in the Son of His love, and so divine was the Son, that "he thought it not a prize to be gained to be equal with God."

The character of Jesus is the "all" of God. Being God, He is God eternally and inherently—without cause, without beginning, without mutation, beyond measure, and without end.

Thinking upon the grace, the goodness, the greatness, and the glory of Jesus, we say, "Great is the Lord and greatly to be praised."

Now, from this great God, actually made flesh, really manifest in the Lord Jesus Christ, we have:

5. AN AMBASSADORIAL ASSIGNMENT: Paul teaches us that the love of Christ constrains Christians, that "all things are of God, who hath reconciled us to himself by Jesus Christ," that God has given to Christians the ministry of reconciliation, and has committed unto them the word of reconciliation (II Corinthians 5:19). And Christians are ambassadors for Christ. "Now then we are ambassadors for Christ, . . ." (II Corinthians 5:20).

Our assignment from our great God, since we are ambassadors for Christ, is to be great Christians for Him—Christians who will weigh at all places and at all times sixteen ounces to the pound on God's scales and measure thirty-six inches to the yard by God's measuring rod, recalling often Jeremiah's words:

Thus saith the LORD, Let not the wise man glory in his wisdom, neither let the mighty man glory in his might, let not the rich man glory in his riches: But let him that glorieth glory in this, that he understandeth and knoweth me, that I am the LORD which exercise lovingkindness, judgment, and righteousness, in the earth; for in these things I delight, saith the LORD (Jeremiah 9:23–24).

Our assignment from God is that in Christian living we should ever be magnificent and never mediocre. God never meant that we should trickle along in service as feeble rills when we can flow as rivers. For us He has rebuke if we have incandescent light powers, and make candle light; if we have pipe organ abilities, and make wheezy saxophone music; if we have locomotive abilities, and do pushcart work; if we have powers to run, and creep along like the sluggard, reluctant to lay hold upon the plow handles; if we have opportunity to bear fruit, and have only leaves; if we have the chance to be giants, achieving greatly, and are puny pigmies piddling potter clay in the face of peaks that dare the pilgrim feet of spiritual pioneers.

George Eliot, speaking of Amos Barton, said something which is, I fear, descriptive of many today: "It was not his nature to be superlative in anything, unless, indeed, he was superlatively middling, the quintessential extract of mediocrity."

I had in mind how far short many Christians fall in meeting their ambassadorial assignments when I preached to my people once on "Bantam Baptists." I could talk (with tears, too) about midget Methodists, pewter Presbyterians, lilliputian Lutherans, puny Pentecostals, miniature Mennonites, diminutive Disciples, and effervescing Episcopalians—because there are many mediocrities among members of all our churches.

Owen Meredith, though he had not mediocrity in mind but only criticism of Eugene de Luvois, in "Lucile," warned us against mediocrity and the menace thereof in these words:

> Down the path of life that led nowhere he trod,
>   Where his whims were his guides,
> And his will was his god,
>   And his pastime his purpose.

What would you think of Beethoven who could make surging seas of tone subservient to his rod, if he were always twanging away on a jew's harp, making mournful monotony of jangling inharmony?

What praise would come to Henry Grady, with power to bathe two antagonistic sections in fraternal light in twenty minutes, if, with national matters of worth in the balance, he would do nothing but recite Mother Goose rhymes? What praise would have Michael Angelo deserved who could "raise children unto God from the sterile womb of stone" had he whittled away with a penknife on soft wood? What would the world have thought of Milton, described as "the tireless blind eagle of the poetic world," had he prostituted his great mind to jest only? What profit would the world have received from Browning had he made his pen to write jingles? What poetic enrichment would have come from Keats had he used his pen to draw figures of fairies in the evanescent frost on a windowpane?

Our ambassadorial assignment *from* God is to be great *for* God. If we will heed and put into deeds the words of Jesus, we will achieve greatness.

> But Jesus called them unto him, and said, Ye know that the princes of the Gentiles exercise dominion over them, and they that are great exercise authority upon them. But it shall not be so among you: but whosoever will be great among you, let him be your minister (Matthew 20:25–26).

President William DeWitt Hyde of Bowdoin College, Maine, tells young people how to live to be great for God: "Live in the *active* rather than the passive voice, intent upon what you can do rather than upon what may happen to you. Live in the *indicative* mood, not the subjunctive, concerned with facts as they are rather than as they might be. Live in the *present* tense, concentrating upon the duty at hand, without regrets for the past or worry about the future. Live in the *first person,* criticizing yourself rather than condemning others. Live in the *singular number,* caring more for the approval of your own conscience than for popularity with the many."

God is abroad in His chariot of gravity. God hides in the conservation of energy. God camps in molecular forces. But God's power in our earth is highest and divinest in a dedicated human being, without which dedication to God no human being can claim greatness.

Our ambassadorial assignment from God is to present our bodies to God as channels through which the divine shall become articulate —to glorify God in our bodies and in our spirits, which are God's (I Corinthians 6:20), to remember that our bodies are not for fornication, but for the Lord—and the Lord for the body (I Corinthians 6:13), knowing assuredly that the body is the temple of the Holy Ghost (I Corinthians 6:19).

> I beseech you therefore, brethren, by the mercies of God, that ye present your bodies a living sacrifice, holy, acceptable unto God, which is your reasonable service (Romans 12:1).

> Let not sin therefore reign in your mortal body, that ye should obey it in the lusts thereof. Neither yield ye your members as instruments of unrighteousness unto sin: but yield yourselves unto God, as those that are alive from the dead, and your members as instruments of righteousness unto God (Romans 6:12–13).

> We are troubled on every side, yet not distressed; we are perplexed, but not in despair; Persecuted, but not forsaken; cast down, but not destroyed; Always bearing about in the body the dying of the Lord Jesus, that the life also of Jesus might be made manifest in our body. For we which live are alway delivered unto death for Jesus' sake, that the life also of Jesus might be made manifest in our mortal flesh (II Corinthians 4:8–11).

Our ambassadorial assignment from God is to yield ourselves and our all in complete surrender to Jesus Christ.

God, through the Apostle Paul, would have us know ". . . what is the riches of the glory of this mystery among the Gentiles; which is Christ in you, the hope of glory: Whom we preach, warning every man, and teaching every man in all wisdom; that we may present every man perfect in Christ Jesus:" (Colossians 1:27–28).

For Christ is the power of God and the wisdom of God in the entirety of man's being and life (I Corinthians 1:24). Christ masters intellect. Christ strengthens the emasculated will. Christ cures vacillation. Some men, passion-driven, are like wind-driven leaves. Some men and women, hurt by hereditary tendencies, are as mercurial as

air. Others born strong, by misuse of the will or by the use of nar-
cotics or alcoholics, weaken the will. But Christ is the power of God
to master sin, to break the fetters of evil habits. Christ is the power of
God to rid life of the imperfection and intermittency that have
plagued it often. Christ is the power of God to make real in men's
experiences these precious words: "... they ... shall know that I am
the LORD, when I have broken the bands of their yoke, ..." (Ezekiel
34:27). Christ is the power of God to make real in human life the
words of God written by Isaiah: "Fear not, thou worm Jacob, and
ye men of Israel; ... I will make thee a new sharp threshing instrument having teeth: thou shalt thresh the mountains, and beat them
small, and shalt make the hills as chaff ... and thou shalt rejoice in
the LORD, ..." (Isaiah 41:14–16).

"Christ in you the hope of glory." Not just future glory in heaven,
where the redeemed will behold Christ's glory, but the glory of
Christly character here and now.

Christ is the wisdom of God to deliver us from the smiling ease
with which faith in eternal things is thrown off, and doubts or lesser
truths grinningly taken on.

Christ is the wisdom of God to bring deliverance from the intellectual conceit which is unaware of the rattle of its dry bones.

Christ is the wisdom of God to avert the tragedy of contracting
spiritual boundaries, while intellectual frontiers are extended.

Christ is the wisdom of God to save men from the superficial
mental illumination that lacks the urge of sacrificial passion.

Christ is the wisdom of God to make real Christ's enunciation of
himself within the precincts of human personality.

In Christ is redemption. "In whom we have redemption through
his blood, even the forgiveness of sins:" (Colossians 1:14).

In Christ is the righteousness of God. "For he hath made him to
be sin for us, who knew no sin; that we might be made the righteousness of God in him" (II Corinthians 5:21).

In Christ is rootage. "In whom are hid all the treasures of wisdom
and knowledge" (Colossians 2:3).

In Christ is perfection. ". . . every man perfect in Christ Jesus" (Colossians 1:28).

In Christ is completion. "For in him dwelleth all the fullness of the Godhead bodily. And ye are complete in him, which is the head of all principality and power" (Colossians 2:9–10).

Thus we see the gravity and glory of accepting our ambassadorial assignment to yield ourselves, with our diverse temperaments, completely to the Christ who "takes the sanguine soul and adds depths to its hopefulness; and the choleric soul, and infuses patience into its passion; and the phlegmatic soul, and kindles its orderliness into ardor; and the melancholy soul, and leads it from brooding meditation forth to joy."

I am right now, and every man is right always, who teaches you to know and urges you to believe that only in Christ Jesus can you measure up to the fullness of your possibilities. Only He who knows your powers knows their possibilities. Only He who fashioned your life can tell the high and holy purpose to which it may be given.

And if men yield not themselves completely to Christ, they are as foolish as the tree which, if it had a tongue, would say: "I should be fruitful, but I can't be bothered with rootage in the soil or sap in my body."

OR as foolish as the field which says: "I want to produce harvests, but I rebel against the sun, the rain, the seed and the plough."

OR as foolish as the locomotive which says: "I must be powerful to pull loaded cars, but I see no sense in fire and steam."

OR as foolish as the automobile which says: "I need to travel, but I refuse to use gas and the highway."

OR as foolish as the light bulb which says: "With my carbon filament, I need to shine and dispel darkness, but I will have nothing to do with the electric current."

OR as foolish as the ship which declares: "I have cargoes to carry, but I will remain in dry dock and have nothing to do with the sea."

OR as foolish as the head which says: "I want to be intelligent, but I have no place in the skull for brains."

OR as foolish as the human body which says: "I want to be

healthy and strong, but I will have nothing to do with blood and muscles."

So I would ask you to have purpose to be great for God—to be united with the Lord as branch *with* tree, to draw your power from God as branch *from* tree, to bear fruit for God as the branch united with the tree, remembering that Jesus said: "Herein is my Father glorified, that ye bear much fruit; . . ." (John 15:8),—not just "fruit," nor *"more* fruit," but *"much* fruit." Then we can, redeemed by Christ, say with Christ, "I have glorified thee on the earth: . . ." (John 17:4).

VII

Jesus Coming to Earth Again

Which also said, Ye men of Galilee, why stand ye gazing up into heaven? this same Jesus, which is taken up from you into heaven, shall so come in like manner as ye have seen him go into heaven (Acts 1:11).

For the Lord himself shall descend from heaven with a shout, with the voice of the archangel, and with the trump of God: and the dead in Christ shall rise first: Then we which are alive and remain shall be caught up together with them in the clouds, to meet the Lord in the air: and so shall we ever be with the Lord. Wherefore, comfort one another with these words (I Thessalonians 4:16–18).

As to Christ's Second Coming, let us consider the:

1. REALITY OF HIS RETURN: No one can read and believe the Bible and not believe in the Second Coming of Christ—when "... the Lord himself shall descend from heaven with a shout, with the voice of the archangel, and with the trump of God: ..." (II Thessalonians 4:16)—when the same Jesus who was taken up from the disciples into heaven will so come in like manner as they saw him go into heaven (Acts 1:11). This is the personal, literal, visible return of the Lord Jesus Himself—not some new movement for the uplift of humanity, not some sweeping revival, not some gifts from Christ, not some catastrophe when God makes the wrath of man to praise Him. As Jesus went away, so will He come. They saw Him leave. They will see Him return. "Behold, he cometh with clouds; and every eye shall see him, ..." (Revelation 1:7). As all the predictions regarding

His first advent, when the world coldly received Him as a babe on a pallet of straw, were literally fulfilled, so shall all the predictions regarding His Second Coming be just as literally fulfilled.

Clearly, definitely, unmistakably, is the Second Coming taught in the Word of God. Only the doctrine of the Atonement is a more prominent Bible truth than the truth concerning the return of the Lord Jesus. In the New Testament, the Second Coming is mentioned 318 times. When the First Coming is mentioned one time, the Second Coming is mentioned eight times. Only by ignorant spiritualizing, or carelessly ignoring or looking upon these passages as interpolations, or by wrenching language out of its setting and rendering it meaningless, can one throw out of court the mass of evidence that Scripture presents. Christ's promise to return is the promise of promises —the crown and consummation of all promises. It is the coronation of all evangelistic hopes, the consummation of prophecy. Christ's promise is unmistakably divine, true, final. He is coming!

Nature and grace alike proclaim a returning glorified Messiah. Nature calls for Him to rectify her unveiling disorders, to repair her shattered structures, to restore her oppressed energies, to verify her sublime testimony to the Creator, so long questioned and overlooked. But grace sends forth a mightier call. If the whole creation groans and travails together in pain for the manifestation of the son of God —how much more those sons of God themselves. As we have whole chapters—Matthew 24, Luke 21, Mark 13—given over to the teaching of the Second Coming, so we have whole books, such as First and Second Thessalonians, devoted to this important subject.

The first Epistle to the Thessalonians is the first written and deals with the truths God would first have taught. Man teaches the Second Coming of the Lord last. Many churches today consider it *incidental*. The churches of the first century considered it *fundamental*. They were certain about the certainty of it. Men think often of Jesus' birth, of His life, of His crucifixion—and many biographies are written. Men think often of Jesus' resurrection, His ascension. We have days to celebrate these great events. But no one has ever suggested to have a day set apart to remember that He is coming again.

Yet His coming again is the next great event in the life of the Son of God. While it is perfectly scriptural to think of all the great facts connected with our salvation as wrought out by Him in the past, the Holy Spirit directs the attention of all believers to the future, and assures us that He is coming again.

To one who accepts the authority of the Scriptures, the testimony of Jesus to His own Second Coming is of outstanding significance. What Jesus said in self-disclosure is of utmost importance. Note how total was the teaching of Christ about Himself. There are 316 separate items of teaching by our Lord. There are 198 items which are about His own person. This degree of self emphasis is amazing. When we study the 198 references to Christ, made by Himself, we find 130 contain specific emphasis upon His own person. These statements reveal the self-consciousness of Jesus.

To get the quickest contact with our Lord's thought about Himself, let us classify in groups:

(1) Jesus spoke of Himself as "the Son of Man" forty-four times.

(2) He called God "My Father" in an exclusive sense twenty times.

(3) He affirmed His unique and exclusive relationship to God ten times.

(4) He pointed to His death, as divinely ordained or having redemptive significance, twenty-five times.

(5) He fore-announced His resurrection from the dead seventeen times.

(6) He promised to be spiritually present while physically absent from His disciples three times.

(7) He set up His person as the supreme motive of life, calling men to do and to suffer in His name and for his sake, seventeen times.

(8) He claimed supreme moral and religious authority thirty-three times.

(9) He claimed to be the final Judge who would determine the everlasting destiny of men twelve times.

(10) He claimed or exercised authority over nature and manifested supernatural knowledge forty-three times.

(11) He rejoiced when men believed in Him and grieved in their unbelief four times.

(12) He accepted the title "Son of God" nine times.

(13) He claimed the title of "Son of God" three times.

(14) Five times He affirmed He held a unique position as the Lord and Master of men.

(15) Forty-four times He claimed for Himself supreme significance as one in whose person centered the ultimate purpose of God.

Concerning the Second Coming, let us think of:

2. THE REASON:

But I would not have you to be ignorant, brethren, concerning them which are asleep, that ye sorrow not, even as others which have no hope (I Thessalonians 4:13).

The reason is that light may be shed upon the death of the believers and that hope may live in the Christian heart. God does not want us to be ignorant. The Bible is written that we may not be ignorant of great things we need to know.

Six times in the New Testament, Paul says: "I would not have you to be ignorant."

Now I would not have you ignorant, brethren, that oftentimes I purposed to come unto you, (but was let hitherto,) that I might have some fruit among you also, even as among other Gentiles (Romans 1:13).

Moreover, brethren, I would not that ye should be ignorant, how that all our fathers were under the cloud, and all passed through the sea; (I Corinthians 10:1).

Now concerning spiritual gifts, brethren, I would not have you ignorant (I Corinthians 12:1).

For we would not, brethren, have you ignorant of our trouble which came to us in Asia, that we were pressed out of measure, above strength, insomuch that we despaired even of life: (II Corinthians 1:8).

> For I would not, brethren, that ye should be ignorant of this mystery, lest ye should be wise in your own conceits; that blindness in part is happened to Israel, until the fulness of the Gentiles be come in (Romans 11:25).

And God would not have us to be ignorant of the Second Coming of Christ and all the signs and events related thereunto.

> But I would not have you to be ignorant, brethren, concerning them which are asleep, that ye sorrow not, even as others which have no hope. For if we believe that Jesus died and rose again, even so them also which sleep in Jesus will God bring with him. For this we say unto you by the word of the Lord, that we which are alive and remain unto the coming of the Lord shall not prevent them which are asleep (I Thessalonians 4:13-15).

It is terrible to be ignorant of some great things. To know botany and be ignorant of Jesus—the Lily of the Valley. To know astronomy and be ignorant of Jesus—the Bright and Morning Star. To know biology and not know the life of Jesus. To know the ages of rocks—and be ignorant of the Rock of Ages. To know mathematics and be ignorant of how to add to faith virtue, knowledge, temperance, patience, godliness, kindness, love. To know about winds and be victims of passions greater than they. To have one's name written on checks and not on the Lamb's Book of Life. To be ignorant of the Second Coming is tragic.

Now think of:

3. THE RETURN: "The Lord himself shall descend from heaven." There will be no substitute. The One who comes is none other than the Lord Jesus Christ. As the first coming was literal in every sense, so his second coming will be literal in every sense. There will be a personal, visible, bodily, glorious re-appearing of Jesus Christ.

(A) *Christ's spiritual presence is not the Second Coming,* for the Bible says: "The Lord Himself." Christ's presence is a reality, but that is distinct from His visible second coming. If His second coming is spiritual, then the same law of interpretation will make the first coming spiritual. "Every eye (not every mind) shall see him."

(B) *Death is not the Second Coming,* for the Bible says: "The Lord Himself." When a Christian dies, Christ does not descend from heaven with a shout. No dead person arises. Nobody is caught up in the clouds. Nobody meets the Lord in the air. No such events take place until Christ returns. No such events occur at death. Therefore, the Second Coming can not mean death. Substitute the word DEATH in Philippians 3:20 and in Matthew 16:28 and see how ridiculous the statement and how nonsensical the teaching that the death of a Christian is the Second Coming of Christ. "For our conversation is in Heaven; from whence also we look for (death) the Lord Jesus Christ." No! ". . . from whence we look for the Saviour, the Lord Jesus Christ."

". . . There be some standing here, which shall not taste of death, until they see (death) coming in his kingdom." Nonsense! Death and Christ are not synonymous. ". . . till they see the Son of man coming in his kingdom."

(C) *Conversion is not the Second Coming of Christ,* for the Bible says: "The Lord Himself." The regeneration of a sinner is as the wind. "The wind bloweth where it listeth, and thou hearest the sound thereof, but canst not tell whence it cometh, and whither it goeth: so is every one that is born of the Spirit" (John 3:8). But this is the first event in a sinner becoming a Christian. Glorious it is when a sinner is saved—when drunkards become sober, when infidels become believers, when liars become truthful, when people born once are born again. But the salvation of a sinner is not the Second Coming.

(D) *Great events in history are not the Second Coming of Christ,* for the Bible says: "The Lord Himself."

Pentecost is not the substitute for the Coming of Christ, even though there are those who say that the predictions regarding Christ's return were fulfilled on that day. Many of the promises regarding the Second Coming were made after the day of Pentecost, when the Holy Spirit came. And none of the events of I Thessalonians 4:16-17 occurred on the Day of Pentecost. On that momentous day, there was no resurrection of the dead, no believers caught up in the clouds to meet the Lord in the air. The Lord *Himself* is coming bodily, visibly, really, actually, corporeally, gloriously, personally. More startling than the scenes of Pentecost, more momentous than the fall of Jerusalem, more significant than the indwelling of the Spirit, more beautiful than the conversion of a sinner, more to be desired than our departure to be with the Lord will be the literal, visible, bodily return of Christ.

When Christ comes, there will be:

4. THE RESURRECTION: "... the dead in Christ shall rise first:" (I Thessalonians 4:16).

Those who die out of Christ are not blessed and holy. They must stay in their graves another one thousand years. Then after the tribulation period and after the millennium, they will be raised and brought in judgment before the Great White Throne where they will receive the condemnation of hell.

> Blessed and holy is he that hath part in the first resurrection: on such the second death hath no power, but they shall be priests of God and of Christ, and shall reign with him a thousand years (Revelation 20:6).

> ... Blessed are the dead which die in the Lord ... (Revelation 14:13).

Dr. Herschel Ford says: "There are sleeping Christians in many different places of the earth. The majority of them are in man-made graves. However, many Christians have gone down into the seas ... many have been burned to death ... some have been lost in the wild places of the earth, and their bones have been picked clean by the birds of the air ... some have suffered and died in the deserts and their bones have been left to bleach in the broiling sun ... some have been torn to pieces in explosions ... some have flown away in airplanes and have never been found. None of this matters to Jesus for He knows everything. He knows where they are and He will show forth his power over death when He comes, for His loved ones will rise from everywhere and not one of them shall be lost."

When I attend the funeral of a Christian, I can truly say to him,

"Good-bye, I will see you with Jesus after a little while." We can say this of all who know Jesus, for we know that it is well with them.

Now, when the dead are taken up, this is the first resurrection—it is not a resurrection *of* the dead but a resurrection *from* the dead. The lost dead will be left in their graves, but the saved ones will be raised incorruptible.

There will be order and program in this resurrection from the dead. Paul outlines this order: "But every man in his own order: Christ the first fruits; afterward they that are Christ's at his coming" (I Corinthians 15:23).

Christ, the first fruits. Then they that are Christ's at His coming. The victory of I Corinthians 15:54-58 will be accomplished:

So when this corruptible shall have put on incorruption, and this mortal shall have put on immortality, then shall be brought to pass the saying that is written, Death is swallowed up in victory. O death, where is thy sting? O grave, where is thy victory? The sting of death is sin; and the strength of sin is the law. But thanks be to God, which giveth us the victory through our Lord Jesus Christ. Therefore, my beloved brethren, be ye stedfast, unmovable, always abounding in the work of the Lord, forasmuch as ye know that your labor is not in vain in the Lord.

Don't overlook:

5. THE RAPTURE:

Then we which are alive and remain shall be caught up together with them in the clouds, to meet the Lord in the air: and so shall we ever be with the Lord (I Thessalonians 4:17).

Every Christian on the earth will hear the commanding shout and will rise up to meet Him. The saved will be taken away before the Great Tribulation overtakes a godless world. The unsaved will be left on earth to go through that awful period. Whether one has been saved a long or a short time, every Christian will be caught up. The living Christians and the dead Christians shall be caught up together and taken away.

Philip was caught away in the Book of Acts:

And when they were come up out of the water, the Spirit of the
Lord caught away Philip, that the eunuch saw him no more: and he
went his way rejoicing (Acts 8:39).

This rapture of the living Christians will be simultaneous with
the resurrection of the righteous dead. Paul is particular to say that
"we who are alive," we who are left unto the coming of the Lord,
shall in no wise precede them that are fallen asleep. These "fallen
asleep" are the dead Christians who are raised in the first resurrection.
Both will be translated together—and will meet the descending Lord
in the air. The rapture of the living Christians will be preceded by a
"change" in their condition. "Behold, I shew you a mystery; We shall
not all sleep, but we shall all be changed" (I Corinthians 15:51). It
will be a change from corruption to incorruption. "For this corruptible must put on incorruption, and this mortal must put on immortality" (I Corinthians 15:53). And all this will take place "in a
moment, in the twinkling of an eye, at the last trump."

After the Rapture, there will be:

6. THE REUNION: We shall be caught up together. Together!
That is just another way of spelling re-union. If we are not to be re-
united to our redeemed loved ones—those whom we have loved and
lost—then for what purpose is this Scripture? When would there be
any comfort? When would there be any consolation? This epistle
was written that Christians sorrow not as those who have no hope.

As Jacob saw Joseph and was with him after twenty years, so shall
we be re-united with our redeemed loved ones. As Naomi was known
when she went home again from the land of Moab, so shall we be
known in the reunion at Christ's coming again.

We read in the first book of the Bible:

"Abraham died and was gathered to his people";

"Isaac died and was gathered to his people";

"Jacob died and was gathered to his people."

"He died in a good old age and was gathered to his people and
they buried him."

What people? Their friends, their comrades, their old com-
panions.

"Gathered unto his people" can hardly mean burial with his people, for the burial is mentioned after it. It comes between the dying and the burial. And we note that when the time of Moses' death had come this phrase is solemnly used: "The Lord said unto him, Get thee up into the mountain and die in the mount, *and be gathered to thy people!*"

Now, Miriam was already buried in the distant desert. Aaron's body lay on the slopes of Mount Hor. The little mother who made the ark of bulrushes long ago found a grave in the brick fields of Egypt.

Do the words teach that Moses came back to his people in this life all unseen when he was "gathered to his people"? Did the expression mean and does it mean that he came back to Miriam's body in the desert and to Aaron's body asleep on Mount Hor and that he lay down again by the side of the little mother in the brick fields of Egypt? No—never. Since he was to *die* and *then,* after dying, be "gathered to his people," it means that into the glory whence they had gone, he was to see them and be with them once again, and *know* them.

Then, without doubt, there will be:

7. THE RECOGNITION: "So shall we be forever with the Lord." At the second advent of the Lord Jesus, there will be a glorious reunion of the redeemed—a reunion made wonderful by recognition.

In all lands, in all ages, under all forms of religion, the fact of recognition in the future world is received. Is it God implanted? Then it is rightfully implanted.

Cicero who lived before Christ's day said: "Oh, glorious day when I shall retire from this low and sordid scene to associate with the divine assemblage of departed spirits . . . with my dear Cato, the best of sons and the most faithful of men. It was my sad fate to lay his body on the funeral pile. If I seemed to bear his death with fortitude it was by no means because I did not feel sensibly the loss I had sustained. It was because I was supported by the consoling reflection that we should not be long separated."

Homer, great man to the Greeks, tells of Ulysses meeting his mother in the spirit world and recognizing her. Virgil represents Aeneas as meeting with his friends over there and talking with them. Socrates was nerved to drink the hemlock because of the thought of meeting the friends who had gone before.

Notice David. There is a sick child in the house of David the king. He sits weeping in the deep shadows. He does not eat; his hunger has been swallowed up in grief too deep for words. He cannot sleep. Nature's great balm that "knits up the raveled sleeve of care" has fled from his eyes. David lies prostrate on his face, until the palace seems a house of many dirges, a house of gloom. What are all these courtly attendants when none of them can cool the fever fires in the body of the child? What are victorious armies when all the soldiers in his kingdom cannot make one little fluttering heart grow stronger? What are conquered provinces when all the revenue cannot buy away the grim figure of death from the bedside of the babe that is sick unto death?

A week passes by, dragging its weary length along. Then there is a great silence in the house. The shutters are closed. People talk in whispers and walk on tiptoe. Then in that great house two little eyelids are gently closed; two little hands are folded over a little bosom that heaves not a sigh; two little feet are at rest; one little heart is forever still.

Then the servants, hushed, awed and hesitant, come to speak the sad tidings to David, the king. But they can not make up their minds to tell him—and at the door they stand, whispering. David hears them and, looking up, asks: "Is the child dead?" "Yes, he is dead!" David rises, washes himself, puts on new apparel, and sits down to eat.

What power hushed that tempest? What strength has lifted up that king whom grief had dethroned? What lifted him from the ashes and gave him the oil of joy for mourning? It was the thought that he would come again into the possession of his child. No grave diggers could hide him. The wintry blasts of death could not put out that bright light. In that fair city where the hoofs of the pale horse never strike the pavement, he would clasp his lost treasure. So David wipes the tears, chokes back his grief and exclaims: "I shall go to him." What, let us ask, would it mean to David to go to his child if he did not know him?

This meeting of redeemed loved ones and friends is one of the many glorious hopes of the resurrection at the return of the Lord. We shall know those who have gone before. This is the glorious hope of the resurrection at the return of the Lord.

> For we know in part, and we prophesy in part.
> For now we see through a glass, darkly; but then face to face: now I know in part; but then shall I know even as also I am known (I Corinthians 13:9, 12).

> Beloved, now are we the sons of God, and it doth not yet appear what we shall be: but we know that, when he shall appear, we shall be like him; for we shall see him as he is. And every man that hath this hope in him purifieth himself, even as he is pure (I John 3:2-3).

It is not strange that the Apostle said, "*Comfort ye one another with these words.*" Surely it is most comforting. And the comfort is a fountain *in* which and *at* which there is no drouth.

Let us give thought to the:

8. REIGN OF JESUS ON EARTH: This is no incident nor accident, but the purpose of God. This kingdom, ordained from the beginning, is no post-creation after-thought of God but a pre-creation thought in His mind from all eternity.

Ordained from the beginning, this reign of Jesus on this earth is the green, flower-scented oasis in the desert of Time. Purposed of God, this kingdom reign of Christ is not heaven—as some seem to think. But is not heaven the culmination of Time? Is heaven not beyond the kingdom—when Time is no more? When the judgment of the Great White Throne is passed and the eternal ages have been flung open. That, as Dr. Len G. Broughton wisely says, is heaven. "And this gospel of the kingdom shall be preached in all the world for a witness unto all nations; and then shall the end come" (Matthew 24:14).

Hear the prophet Zechariah:

And his feet shall stand in that day upon the mount of Olives, which is before Jerusalem on the east, and the mount of Olives shall cleave in the midst thereof toward the east and toward the west, and there shall be a very great valley; and half of the mountain shall remove toward the north, and half of it toward the south. And ye shall flee to the valley of the mountains; for the valley of the mountains shall reach unto Azal: yea, ye shall flee, like as ye fled from before the earthquake in the days of Uzziah king of Judah; and the Lord my God shall come, and all the saints with thee (Zechariah 14:4-5).

This refers to the earthly kingdom. Thus shall the King come—and men shall see Him. And not Him only but all the vast domain of His kingdom. The devil shall be chained and sealed in a pit to deceive the nations no more until the thousand years are past.

The kingdoms of the earth, now glaring at each other across chasms of suspicion and ill will, shall learn war no more—shall be held together by Jesus Christ, who shall reign in all the affairs of the earth—and we shall have a new earth. This is the Word of God who says "I make all things new." Jesus shall come and set His face against the powers of darkness to reign over the united kingdoms of earth.

This kingly administration of Jesus will be personal, and not just spiritual.

Dr. Len G. Broughton says:

Language cannot be made any plainer than that which is used descriptive of Christ's second coming and the establishment of His kingdom. If His second coming is spiritual, and the kingdom which He is coming to establish is likewise spiritual, then the same law of interpretation will make His first coming spiritual. Oh, what a calamity this would be! It would rob the manger of its poetry and pathos. It would stop the song of the angel chorus on the morning of his birth. It would annul the matchless teaching, by precept and example, of our blessed Lord. It would climb the slopes of Calvary and hide away the blood of the covenant. It would pass over as a myth the story of the sepulchre, and frown with scorn upon the glories of Olivet. If the second coming of Jesus is spiritual the sublimest picture contained in the gallery of inspired truth is destroyed, that picture of the disciples assembled together on the day of His ascension when the invisible chariot of God, let down from heaven, caught up the Saviour, and bore Him away to His far away home in the glory.

When Jesus comes, the pattern prayer of the saints, "Thy kingdom come, thy will be done on earth as it is in heaven," will be heard. Jesus, the rejected, will seize the reigns of government and rule in beneficent power and victory.

After the rapture of the living Christians and the resurrection of the dead Christians—all of whom shall be given glorified bodies as they are caught up together to meet the Lord in the air—the unrighteous dead and the unrighteous living are left. The unrighteous dead shall sleep on in their graves until the thousand years of the reign of Christ is past.

Immediately following the rapture of the saints at the first is the period of THE great tribulation. The Devil is in absolute control. The Holy Spirit's day has passed. Christ has not yet come to earth. He is in the clouds with His saints from whence they enter into heaven. This is followed by the "judgment-seat-of-Christ" judgment, where rewards are given and ranks assigned.

But on the earth is not only the absence of the Holy Spirit, but the presence of the Devil.

Therefore rejoice, ye heavens, and ye that dwell in them. Woe to the inhabiters of the earth and of the sea! for the devil is come down unto you, having great wrath, because he knoweth that he hath but a short time (Revelation 12:12).

The Devil was first cast out of the Mount of God:

By the multitude of thy merchandise they have filled the midst of thee with violence, and thou hast sinned: therefore I will cast thee as profane out of the mountain of God: and I will destroy thee, O covering cherub, from the midst of the stones of fire (Ezekiel 28:16).

The Devil was next cast out into the air:

Wherein in time past ye walked according to the course of this world, according to the prince of the power of the air, the spirit that now worketh in the children of disobedience: (Ephesians 2:2).

When Jesus comes "in the air," the Devil is cast down to the earth. "Inhabiters of the earth, the Devil is come down to you." And, because of the Devil having power and great wrath, utterly unopposed, knowing this time is short, will rule with a high hand.

Describing this terrible tribulation, John writes in the Revelation:

And in those days shall men seek death, and shall not find it; and shall desire to die, and death shall flee from them (Revelation 9:6).

And concerning those days, Matthew writes:

For then shall be great tribulation, such as was not since the beginning of the world to this time, no, nor ever shall be. And except those days should be shortened, there should no flesh be saved: but for the elect's sake those days shall be shortened (Matthew 24:21–22).

This tribulation will make the worst famine seem as a feast, the world's worst wars seem as children's parties. But when Christ and his bride are united in the air then Christ will come to earth and the Devil be cast into the bottomless pit.

Here he must stay for one thousand years.

And I saw an angel come down from heaven, having the key of the bottomless pit and a great chain in his hand. And he laid hold on the dragon, that old serpent, which is the Devil, and Satan, and bound him a thousand years, and cast him into the bottomless pit, and shut him up, and set a seal upon him, that he should deceive the nations no more, till the thousand years should be fulfilled: and after that he must be loosed a little season. And I saw thrones, and they sat upon them, and judgment was given unto them: and I saw the souls of them that were beheaded for the witness of Jesus, and for the word of God, and which had not worshipped the beast, neither his image, neither had received his mark upon their foreheads, or in their hands; and they lived and reigned with Christ a thousand years. But the rest of the dead lived not again until the thousand years were finished. This is the first resurrection. Blessed and holy is he that hath part in the first resurrection: on such the second death hath no power, but they shall be priests of God and of Christ, and shall reign with him a thousand years (Revelation 20:1–6).

Since the millennium is to be a time of righteousness and peace, it is absolutely necessary that Satan be removed from the earth. How can you have a golden age without getting rid of the Devil? Satan, too strong to be overcome by any human power, will be locked up by the Omnipotent Christ.

The arrest of Satan before the millennium! Thus the most notable arrest the universe has ever known is here described. An angel makes the arrest. The earth could enjoy no rest with Satan unbound. For one thousand years, "that old serpent which is the devil and Satan," will remain in the prison of the pit. Satan's freedom has filled the earth with disease, death, decay, destruction, sin, sorrow, suffering, pain, pang, groan, moan, tears, tragedy, dying, sighing, crying, war. But during his confinement, the earth will enjoy a Sabbath of rest. A thousand years of peace in a Satanless world! Think of it—and rejoice!

Jesus brings His bride back to the earth and will not allow Satan to roam the earth. Then will come the bridal party to the "new earth."

And the Lord shall be king over all the earth: in that day shall there be one Lord, and his name one (Zechariah 14:9).

His eyes were as a flame of fire, and on his head were many crowns; and he had a name written, that no man knew, but he himself.

And out of his mouth goeth a sharp sword, that with it he should smite the nations: and he shall rule them with a rod of iron: and he treadeth the winepress of the fierceness and wrath of Almighty God. And he hath on his vesture and on his thigh a name written, KING OF KINGS, AND LORD OF LORDS (Revelation 19:12, 15–16).

Satan is silenced. This is what we call the millennium.

It is the answer to the prayer of Christ, which was given as our pattern: "Thy kingdom come, Thy will be done, on earth as in heaven." This could never occur until Satan is out of the way.

With Satan bound, Christ shall sit upon His throne—and rule.

And speak unto him, saying, Thus speaketh the LORD of hosts, saying, Behold the man whose name is The BRANCH; and he shall grow up out of his place, and he shall build the temple of the LORD: even he shall build the temple of the LORD; and he shall bear the glory, and shall sit and rule upon his throne; and he shall be a priest upon his throne: and the counsel of peace shall be between them both (Zechariah 6:12-13).

And the LORD shall be king over all the earth: in that day shall there be one LORD, and his name one (Zechariah 14:9).

Then the moon shall be confounded, and the sun ashamed, when the LORD of hosts shall reign in mount Zion, and in Jerusalem, and before his ancients gloriously (Isaiah 24:23).

And I will cut off the chariot from Ephraim, and the horse from Jerusalem, and the battle bow shall be cut off: and he shall speak peace unto the heathen: and his dominion shall be from sea even to sea, and from the river even to the ends of the earth (Zechariah 9:10). Yea, all kings shall fall down before him: all nations shall serve him (Psalms 72:11).

I saw in the night visions, and, behold, one like the Son of man came with the clouds of heaven, and came to the Ancient of days, and they brought him near before him. And there was given him dominion, and glory, and a kingdom, that all people, nations, and languages, should serve him: his dominion is an everlasting dominion, which shall not pass away, and his kingdom that which shall not be destroyed.

And the kingdom and dominion, and the greatness of the kingdom under the whole heaven, shall be given to the people of the saints of the most High, whose kingdom is an everlasting kingdom, and all dominions shall serve and obey him (Daniel 7:13-14, 27).

He shall be great, and shall be called the Son of the Highest: and the Lord God shall give unto him the throne of his father David: And he shall reign over the house of Jacob for ever; and of his kingdom there shall be no end (Luke 1:32-33).

Therefore being a prophet, and knowing that God had sworn with an oath to him, that of the fruit of his loins, according to the flesh, he would raise up Christ to sit on his throne (Acts 2:30).

If those promises are not fulfilled, then the Word of God is false. But they shall be kept. God's Word is true.

During the thousand years—while Satan is bound and Jesus reigns—justice will prevail without partiality.

Behold, the days come, saith the LORD, that I will raise unto David a righteous Branch, and a King shall reign and prosper, and shall execute judgment and justice in the earth (Jeremiah 23:5).

Behold, a king shall reign in righteousness, and princes shall rule in judgment (Isaiah 32:1).

There will be a new and fruitful earth:

The wilderness and the solitary place shall be glad for them; and the desert shall rejoice, and blossom as the rose. It shall blossom abundantly, and rejoice even with joy and singing: the glory of Lebanon shall be given unto it, the excellency of Carmel and Sharon they shall see the glory of the Lord, and the excellency of our God (Isaiah 35:1-2).

And the desolate land shall be tilled, whereas it lay desolate in the sight of all that passed by. And they shall say, This land that was desolate is become like the garden of Eden; and the waste and desolate and ruined cities are become fenced, and are inhabited (Ezekiel 36:34-35).

Behold, the days come, saith the Lord, that the plowman shall overtake the reaper, and the treader of grapes him that soweth seed; and the mountains shall drop sweet wine, and all the hills shall melt (Amos 9:13).

The ferocious nature of animals and their instincts will be changed:

The wolf also shall dwell with the lamb, and the leopard shall lie down with the kid; and the calf and the young lion and the fatling together; and a little child shall lead them. And the cow and the bear shall feed; their young ones shall lie down together: and the lion shall eat straw like the ox. And the sucking child shall play on the hole of the asp, and the weaned child shall put his hand on the cockatrice's den (Isaiah 11:6–8).

The wolf and the lamb shall feed together, and the lion shall eat straw like the bullock: and dust shall be the serpent's meat. They shall not hurt nor destroy in all my holy mountain, saith the LORD (Isaiah 65:25).

There will be no more war:

And he shall judge among the nations, and shall rebuke many people: and they shall beat their swords into plowshares, and their spears into pruninghooks: nation shall not lift up sword against nation, neither shall they learn war any more (Isaiah 2:4).

Through the years men have talked of "learning war no more" —have talked of the time when the earth would be filled with righteousness and peace. Some men think they can bring about such a desirable age through education, United Nations, social betterment, scientific achievements, reformation, preaching, missionary work, and other human agencies. It will take more than all the things all men can do to straighten this old world out. Human plans and human hands and human powers cannot do it. There is only one—Jesus Christ, to whom God hath given all power in heaven and in earth.

There shall be perfect safety:

And I will make with them a covenant of peace, and will cause the evil beasts to cease out of the land: and they shall dwell safely in the wilderness, and sleep in the woods (Ezekiel 34:25).

But they shall sit every man under his vine and under his fig tree; and none shall make them afraid: for the mouth of the LORD of hosts hath spoken it (Micah 4:4).

There shall be long life:

There shall be no more thence an infant of days, nor an old man that hath not filled his days: for the child shall die an hundred years old; but the sinner being an hundred years old shall be accursed (Isaiah 65:20).

There will be evangelization of the world:

And they shall not teach every man his neighbor, and every man his brother, saying, Know the Lord: for all shall know me, from the least to the greatest (Hebrews 8:11).

For the earth shall be filled with the knowledge of the glory of the LORD, as the waters cover the sea (Habakkuk 2:14).

The saints, even we, shall reign:

Do ye not know that the saints shall judge the world? and if the world shall be judged by you, are ye unworthy to judge the smallest matters? (I Corinthians 6:2).

And the things that thou hast heard of me among many witnesses, the same commit thou to faithful men, who shall be able to teach others also (II Timothy 2:2).

And I saw thrones, and they sat upon them, and judgment was given unto them: and I saw the souls of them that were beheaded for the witness of Jesus, and for the word of God, and which had not worshipped the beast, neither his image, neither had received his mark upon their foreheads, or in their hands; and they lived and reigned with Christ a thousand years (Revelation 20:4).

Jerusalem shall be the center of worship:

Thus saith the LORD of hosts; It shall yet come to pass, that there shall come people, and the inhabitants of many cities: and the inhabitants of one city shall go to another, saying, Let us go speedily to pray before the LORD, and to seek the LORD of hosts: I will go also. Yea, many people and strong nations shall come to seek the LORD of hosts in Jerusalem, and to pray before the LORD. Thus saith the LORD of hosts; In those days it shall come to pass, that ten men shall take

hold out of all languages of the nations, even shall take hold of the
skirt of him that is a Jew, saying, We will go with you: for we have
heard that God is with you (Zechariah 8:20–23).

But in the last days it shall come to pass, that the mountain of the
house of the LORD shall be established in the top of the mountains, and
it shall be exalted above the hills; and people shall flow unto it. And
many nations shall come, and say, Come, and let us go up . . . to the
house of the God of Jacob; and he will teach us of his ways, and we
will walk in his paths: for the law shall go forth of Zion, and the
word of the LORD from Jerusalem (Micah 4:1–2).

For one thousand years, Jesus will place everything good in the
world and keep everything bad out of it. Christ will "appear the
second time without sin, unto salvation"—not tinting the earth and
seas and skies with the transient beauty of the sunrise, but raising
the dead, changing the living, judging the world, glorifying His
people, and establishing His everlasting kingdom of "righteousness,
peace, and joy, in the Holy Ghost."

What our science could not do, He will do. What our theology
and preaching could not do, He will do. What our parliaments and
senates could not do, He will do. What our educational systems
could not do, He will do. What our armies and navies could not do,
He will do.

And that day will be the watcher's looked-for day, the purchaser's
redemption day, the builder's completion day, the husbandman's
harvest day, the servant's reckoning day, the master's pay day, the
Son's manifestation day, the Bride's wedding day, the King's coronation day.

I heard Dr. John Roach Straton in New York once, quoting in
part another, set forth some of the glories of the millennial reign of
Christ in these words:

"Think of the sudden collapse of all the haunts of sin, the root-
ing out of the nests and nurseries of iniquity, the clearing away of
the marshes and bogs of crime, where every type of damning pesti-
lence is bred, and the changes that must hence come;—think of the

summary abolition of all infamous cliques, combinations, and rings, —political rings, whisky rings, municipal rings, state rings, railroad rings, mercantile rings, communistic rings, oath-bound rings, and a thousand kind of other rings—all the children of wickedness, hindering just law, suppressing moral right, crippling honest industry, subsidizing legislation, corrupting the Press, robbing the public treasuries, eating up the gains of honorable occupation, perverting public sentiment, spotting and exorcising men who can not be made the tools of party, transmuting selfish greed and expediency into principle, razing the dominion of virtue and intelligence, subordinating the common weal to individual aggrandisement, and setting all righteous administration at defiance. Think of the universal and invincible dragging forth to divine justice of every blatant infidel, perjurer, liar, profane swearer, drunkard, drunkard-maker, whoremonger, hypocrite, slanderer, trickster, cheat, thief, murderer, trader in uncleanness, truce-breaker, traitor, miser, oppressor of the poor, bribe-taking legislator, time-serving preacher, mal-practitioner, babe-destroyer, friend-robber, office-usurper, peace-disturber, life-embitterer. Think of the instantaneous going forth into all the world of a divine and unerring force, which can not be turned or avoided, but which hews down every fruitless tree, purges away all chaff from every floor, negatives all unrighteous laws, overwhelms all unrighteous traffic, destroys all unrighteous coalitions, burns up every nest of infamy and sin, ferrets out all concealed wickedness, exposes and punishes all empty pretence, makes an end of all unholy business, and puts an effectual stop to all base fashions, all silly conceits, all questionable customs, and all the hollow shams and corrupt show and fastidiousness of what calls itself society, transferring the dominion of the almighty dollars to Almighty Right, and reducing everything in human life, pursuits, manners, and professions to the standard of rigid truth and justice." (From a Sermon by Dr. Straton.)

Give thought as to the end-Time and the:

9. REVEALINGS: I mean by this the signs of the end-time.

(A) There is the Apostasy sign.

Let no man deceive you by any means: for that day shall not come, except there come a falling away first, and that man of sin be revealed, the son of perdition (II Thessalonians 2:3).

And they shall turn away their ears from the truth, and shall be turned unto fables (II Timothy 4:4).

Now the Spirit speaketh expressly, that in the latter times some shall depart from the faith, giving heed to seducing spirits, and doctrines of devils; (I Timothy 4:1).

Dr. John W. Raley, president of Oklahoma Baptist University, said: "We face a problem of paganistic order and pessimistic philosophy. Out of thirty-five outstanding educators in America who were questioned on the question of religion only one revealed a well-defined attitude of loyalty to the Word of God."

Many, by those who chose the livery of heaven to serve the devil, are being led, or misled, along the path of spiritual apostasy into spiritual night. Many doubt and openly repudiate the virgin birth, the blood atonement, the bodily resurrection, the visible return of Jesus, the necessity of the new birth—all of which are the very things that give distinctive reality to the Christian faith as the one and only supernatural, God-given system of religious belief with which this old sin-cursed world has ever been blessed.

(B) *There is the Riotous Revelry sign.*

But as the days of Noe were, so shall also the coming of the Son of man be. For as in the days that were before the flood they were eating and drinking, marrying and giving in marriage, until the day that Noe entered into the ark, And knew not until the flood came, and took them all away; so shall also the coming of the Son of man be (Matthew 24:37-39).

Our amusement world is erotic, neurotic. Much pleasure life is banal and bawdy.

(C) *There is the Moral-Spiritual decay sign.*

This know also, that in the last days perilous times shall come. For men shall be lovers of their own selves, covetous, boasters, proud, blasphemers, disobedient to parents, unthankful, unholy, Without natural affection, truce-breakers, false accusers, incontinent, fierce, despisers of those that are good, Traitors, heady, highminded, lovers of pleasures more than lovers of God; having a form of godliness, but denying the power thereof: from such turn away. For of this sort are they which creep into houses, and lead captive silly women laden with sins, led away with divers lusts, Ever learning, and never able to come to the knowledge of the truth (II Timothy 3:1-7).

(D) *There is the Hunger-Famine sign.*

For nation shall rise against nation, and kingdom against kingdom: and there shall be famines, and pestilences, and earthquakes, in divers places (Matthew 24:7).

The world has never known so much of famine and hunger as it knows now. The mightiest battle of the recent past and of the present is the battle for bread. The wildest cry is the cry of hunger—little children tugging at empty breasts, to whom milk is as nectar and crusts a feast. Men taking their own lives that their families may live is the tragedy of our times, and a sign of His coming.

(E) *There is the Earthquakes sign.*

Earthquakes in several places at the same time. In a few newspapers in recent years, there have been between eighty and ninety reports of earthquakes. A total of 238 earthquakes were reported in three months of a recent year. During the Turkish earthquake that took ten thousand lives and caused millions in damage, that same day there were earthquakes in South Africa, the Carolinas, California, South America. Recently there was a terrible earthquake in Formosa.

(F) *There is the False-Christ sign.*

For many shall come in my name, saying, I am Christ; and shall deceive many (Matthew 24:5).

What reports in the public press have heralded to the world fulfillment of this prophecy? Chiefly, three: the coming forth of Abdul Baha, Agag Khan, and J. Krishnamurti, a trio arising in the East. Some time ago, we read: "Three Persians, of successive generations

—the Bab, the Door; Baha Ullah, the Glory of God; and Abdul Baha, the Branch—all appropriating titles exclusively our Lord's, have founded a sect now exceeding six millions."

"So Abdul Baha's claims logically soar into the fullest Messianism:

> I am all these (earlier Messiahs) together. I supersede all previous teachers. Christ was the highest until I came and now it is the duty of mankind to listen to me, instead of listening to the teachings of those who preceded me.

(G) There is the Distress of Nations sign.

> . . . upon the earth distress of nations, with perplexity (Luke 21:25).

> This know also, that in the last days perilous times shall come (II Timothy 3:1).

The nations are distressed today by external and internal dangers. What are some of these external dangers? Unprecedented preparations for war, overwhelming national debts, and seemingly hopeless recovery.

(H) There is the Scientific-Progress sign.

> But thou, O Daniel, shut up the words, and seal the book, even to the time of the end: many shall run to and fro, and knowledge shall be increased (Daniel 12:4).

When Jesus talked on this earth, a man's tent was His castle and His camel was his touring car. Jesus never saw a gas jet nor an electric lamp. Only one time do we read of his riding. He himself never saw a railroad train, a trolley car, an automobile, a steamship, or an airplane. He who walked in the harvest field never saw a tractor engine, a steam plow, a harvester, a twine binder, a seed sower, or a reaper. He who wrote in the sand never saw a typewriter, a telegraph instrument, a telephone, a radio. He who read the Scripture lesson in the synagogue at Nazareth never read a newspaper, a magazine, or saw a public library or a moving picture. This great teacher never saw a public school. This Great Physician never saw an anaesthetic, a hospital, as we know it, or a Red Cross society. He of the seamless robe never saw a sewing machine. He whose face has been pictured by the artists of every nation never saw a camera, posed for a photograph, or sat for a painting. But now look and think of human progress.

(I) There is the Wars- and Talk-of-Wars sign.

Not only wars. But rumors of wars. The Greek for "rumors" is AKOEE. From that word comes our English word "acoustics." This word is variously translated in the New Testament. It is rendered "report" ("report of him" A.S.V.) in Matthew 4:24:

> And his fame went throughout all Syria: and they brought unto him all sick people that were taken with divers diseases and torments, and those which were possessed with devils, and those which were lunatick, and those that had the palsy; and he healed them.

This word is also rendered "saying" and "hearing," but in the expression "rumors of wars," Jesus meant "news of wars and talks of wars." That meant our age would be increasingly characterized not only by actual war, but also by talk of war. There has not been in all human history such a generation so dominated by the talk of war as this one in which we live.

In 1900–1905, twenty-nine volumes were published on armaments, military acts and sciences and wars.

In 1938, there were sixty-four volumes published on this subject plus about one hundred volumes on the European War.

In the first six months of 1950, as many books were published on war and military science as in the first six years of this century, plus 140 volumes on the late World War.

In addition to all this, we now have frightful terms which the dawn of our century knew nothing of—chemical warfare, biological warfare, aerial warfare, atomic weapons—and all the fearful missiles involved in these areas.

In the New York Times in 1938, there were 530 war lines.

In the New York Times in 1949, there were six thousand war lines.

In the index to the Congressional Record from January 16th to December 31st, 1948, there were six hundred different items alone under the heading "National Defense" and "National Military establishment."

In this same index for the 68th Congress in 1926, there were eighteen references for international peace, world peace, and disarmament.

Our Lord said that toward the end of the age, there would be "talk of war." This prediction has never been so overwhelmingly true as in this very hour.

Let us consider *seriously* the:

10. READINESS:

Then shall two be in the field; the one shall be taken, and the other left. Two women shall be grinding at the mill; the one shall be taken, and the other left. Watch therefore: for ye know not what hour your Lord doth come. But know this, that if the goodman of the house had known in what watch the thief would come, he would have watched, and would not have suffered his house to be broken up. Therefore be ye also ready: for in such an hour as ye think not the Son of man cometh (Matthew 24:40-44).

Be ye also ready, for in such an hour as ye think not the Son of Man cometh.

Then shall the kingdom of heaven be likened unto ten virgins, which took their lamps, and went forth to meet the bridegroom. And five of them were wise, and five were foolish. They were foolish took their lamps, and took no oil with them: but the wise took oil in their vessels with their lamps. While the bridegroom tarried, they all slumbered and slept. And at midnight there was a cry made, Behold, the bridegroom cometh; go ye out to meet him. Then all those virgins arose, and trimmed their lamps. And the foolish said unto the wise, Give us of your oil; for our lamps are gone out. But the wise answered, saying, Not so; lest there be not enough for us and you: but go ye rather to them that sell, and buy for yourselves. And while they went to buy, the bridegroom came; and they that were ready went in with him to the marriage: and the door was shut.

Afterward came also the other virgins, saying, Lord, Lord, open to us. But he answered and said, Verily I say unto you, I know you not. Watch therefore, for ye know neither the day nor the hour wherein the Son of man cometh (Matthew 25:1-13).

The emphasis is on *They that were ready went in.*

Some are not ready for love. Some are not ready for opportunity. Some are not ready for life. Some are not ready for death. Some are not ready for eternity.

Readiness—and "not be ashamed before him at his coming." That is our need. But to have joy when He comes. When He comes, we will be gladly waiting or sadly fearing.

How great was the joy in the Bethany home when they knew the Lord Jesus was coming! Did Martha hope He would not come because she had spring cleaning to do? Did Mary hope He would not come—because she had so many letters to write? Did Lazarus hope He would not come—because he was so engrossed with business? No! It was their *joy* to know the Lord was coming, for Christ put everything right.

By your desire for the appearing of your Lord, you can judge the state of your spiritual life.

The immigrant comes to these shores. He works to earn money to pay the passage of his beloved. When that ship comes in, he is on the dock. When the gangplank is lowered, he is at the barrier waiting for her to come through the customs. That is the attitude the Christian should have toward the coming of his Lord.

Do you want the Lord to come back? If you are an unsaved sinner, you do not want Him to come. You will be left when He appears, because He comes to take those who love Him, who have His Spirit in their hearts, who are His by faith. If you are a backslidden Christian, you do not want Him to come, because you will be embarrassed and ashamed. If the love of the world has grown so warm in your heart that the love of your Lord has grown cold, you do not want Him to come because you are tied up with this world and have no desire to see Him.

Do you want the Lord to come back? John saw all the glories of the end time. Then he cried with heartfelt personal longing, "Even so, Lord Jesus, come quickly."

I want Him to come for a good many reasons. I do not have much hope, so far as this world is concerned, that everything is ever going to be at peace again. I want the Lord to come back because I would like to know my children are safe with Him.

I want Him to come because I am tired of all the chaos, unrest and uncertainty, all the fumblings of government, and the greed and envy of men. I am sickened of pictures of naked babies with swollen stomachs, stretching out thin, emaciated arms for a crust of bread in the streets of the cities of Asia. I am tired of pictures of blasted homes and falling bombs and boys with arms and legs lost on the field of battle. I want the Lord to come because He will set up a reign of righteousness on the earth.

But most of all I want Him to come because I want to see Him. I have never seen Him with these eyes, but with the eyes of faith I saw Him once when I knelt at the old fence corner and trusted Him. Perhaps I haven't always been faithful, but He has been, and I want Him to come because I want to tell Him I love Him. I want Him to come; do you? Then why stand ye gazing up? Witness and watch and work, and some day—pray God some day *soon*—we'll see Him in whom our souls delight, and be like Him forevermore.

> Behold, what manner of love the Father hath bestowed upon us, that we should be called the sons of God: therefore the world knoweth us not, because it knew him not. Beloved, now are we the sons of God, and it doth not yet appear what we shall be: but we know that, when he shall appear, we shall be like him; for we shall see him as he is. And every man that hath this hope in him purifieth himself, even as he is pure (I John 3:1-3).